Beyond broken

Brendan Conboy

Dedication

**To God, the Author of Life, my life,
my protector, provider and deliverer.**

**You have given me the tools and skills to write.
This book exists because of you.**

*You picked up all my pieces
Put me back together
You are the defender of my heart
(Rita Springer)*

Published by
Yellow Dog Publishing

All rights reserved.

First published November 2023

Copyright © Brendan M Conboy 2023
www.brendanconboy.co.uk

Cover photography – Photo Vision
Design - Brendan Conboy

Printed in Great Britain
ISBN 978-1-7393684-3-2

Thanks

To Heather my wife,
life-long companion and friend.
She is my lieutenant on the battlefield,
the soother of my wounds,
my carer when I need to recover,
my aid to understand,
when my brain needs clarity.
She is patient, loving and kind and
helped me immensely to remember
much of the detail of this book.
Her input has enabled me to
tell this story with integrity.
She is more precious than rubies and greatly
VALUED.

Thanks also to my good friend Jason Parker, for
his patience in searching for errors in my writing
and for helping to make this book what it is
today.

About this book

This is my continuing biography, the sequel to
The Golden Thread.

Read this book as a stand-alone book or for the
full picture read the first book first.

Index

I'm Still Valued

I used to climb up mountains
Be the first up to the top
I used to ride a bicycle
But crashing made me stop
When I worked on building sites
I was a beautiful sight
I used to have more energy
When young and oh-so-free
For sixty hours I worked each week
I could manage on six hours sleep
I used to lead the greatest team
Now I'm lonely in my dreams
My brain still thinks the way it did
My body says, "You are not a kid."
I've lost so much of who I was
A broken man now because
My health has just deteriorated
Left me feeling so deflated
I often wonder what to do
I know that I am still valued
Forgetting what has gone before
I know that I'm so capable
I am valued and can do more
As long as I do live and breathe
God still calls me for His need

Life is complicated

My life is complicated and no book will ever allow you to fully understand the things that I have experienced. The last decade has been a battle, an onslaught of one major event after another. These are usually health events that would make some people give up on life. I haven't given up because I am convinced that God still values me and wants to use me. I know that my life has been complicated and readers may like to have some chronological order. This is why I have produced a timeline. I hope that you find it helpful and you can use it as a spoiler for the stories to come.

Timeline of events

2008 – Diagnosed with polycystic kidney disease and heart disease (angina) in the same year.
2012 – Decided to work a two-year exit plan from my position as charity CEO. My mental health deteriorated (depression and anxiety).
2014 – (Feb) Hospital - Surgery for 3 cardio stents.
(Jun/Jul) Wrote my first book, The Golden Thread.

(Nov) Leave The Door charity and start charity consultancy work.

2015 – (Sept) **The Golden Thread (book) published**.

2016 – (Feb) Added to kidney transplant waiting list.

(Aug) Surgery to commence dialysis – **life-threatening complications**.

(Sep) Dialysis commenced.

(Oct) Joined The Shaggy Dog Raconteurs (band) as their drummer.

2017 – (Jul) 1st Transplant call.

2018 – (Jan) 1st Potential living donor.

(Feb) 2nd Transplant call.

(Mar) Clinically depressed and suicidal.

(May) 2nd Potential living donor.

(Jul) God told me that **I'm still valued.**

2019 – (Jan) 3rd Transplant call.

(Feb) 4th Transplant call.

(Feb) 5th Transplant call – Surgery for transplant – **life-threatening complications**.

(Jan) **Issues (book) published**.

(Feb) **My Foundation for Life (book) published.**

2020 – (Mar) Lockdown

(Jun) – Accident – **life-threatening complications**.

(Nov) **Rhyme Time (book) published**.

(Oct) **Invasion of the Mimics (book) published**.

2021 – (Mar) **Land of Make-Believe (book) published.**

(May) Diagnosed with severe Sleep Apnoea.

(May) Hospital - Surgery for 3 more cardio stents.

(Jul) **One God Many Names (book) published**.

(Aug) **The book of Psalms in Rhyme (book) published**.

2022 – (Mar) Hospital - surgery shoulder replacement (following accident).

(Jun) **Legacy of the Mimics (book) published**.

(Jul) Left The Shaggy Dog Raconteurs (band).

(Aug) **Popcorn Poetry (book) published**.

(Nov) 1st Book Blest Christian book festival

(Dec) Back in the hospital with unstable angina.

2023 – (Jan) Heart surgery – Triple bypass – **life-threatening complications**.

(Mar) Chronic kidney infection - Hospital

(Apr) **Half Man Half Poet (book) published**.

Chapter One
Let's get started

Without any doubt, this book has been the most difficult and painful that I have ever written. I started the first draft in February 2022 and eventually, after six rewrites, it went to be edited in October 2023, that's 20 months in total. In my first book, 'The Golden Thread', I talked about some of the amazing, inspirational and motivational stories that have happened during my life thus far. I also mentioned many of the immense struggles and tangible fears, but also how God came into my life in a transformational way. That book ended at the time when I left The Door Youth Project in 2014.

This book is my continuing story, with some slight overlap with the previous one. In this book, I will take you on a different journey of pain and discovery. My physical health has deteriorated in lots of different ways. Some of those underlying issues were anticipated and inevitable, whilst other conditions I've been wrestling with just seemed to come out of nowhere.

The last nine years have been an almost constant battle. I have manoeuvred through life's many combat zones and all of its setbacks. Although there have been times when I felt like giving up, I have fought back, remained positive and become a 'warrior.'

I always say that it is better to be a warrior than a worrier. I don't think adding anxiety into the mix has ever solved a problem. I want to go kicking and screaming into my grave. I want to keep on fighting to the end and hopefully encourage others to do the same. I wouldn't want anyone to give up. I want to try and help everyone to uncover a deeper understanding of what it means to be valued.

Well, that is what I would 'like' to think anyway, but let's be honest here... does anyone really think like that when push comes to shove? There have been times when I have cried with despair and screamed with turmoil. I have walked through the darkest valleys and wanted my life to end. I have experienced a few highs but also encountered the lows, which have been present more often. I have faced an unrealistic amount of trauma and on many occasions questioned God as to why all of this has happened. I have learnt much and I have changed, although I am still far from perfect.

If you can relate to some of what I say... If you have health struggles and feel like giving up, remember this - You are still valued by God and He still wants to use you.

There have been times when I found myself in a hospital and questioned God why I am here. Shortly afterwards, a conversation is usually started with a nurse or another patient about being a Christian. God can and will use you in the strangest of places if you are willing and available to be used. How often do you say, "Here I am Lord wholly available"?

If you think God has given up on you, think again. It is much more likely that it is you who has given up on God. It's easy to feel devalued, discarded and rejected. When we feel this way, we tend to treat God the same, we ignore Him, try things our way and blame God when it all goes wrong. In our devalued state, we devalue the power of God. In our confused minds, we doubt that God cares. In our feelings of rejection, it is so easy to just give up and reject all that you have believed.

14

When my first granddaughter was born, I said that I wanted to be at her wedding when she was married. She is now 12 years old and I still want that. I figure she will not marry for at least 10 years. In the last 10 years, I have brushed with death at least four times, so in reality, the odds are stacked against me. As I think about those odds, I am reminded that in God, *'all things are possible' (Matthew 19:26).*

This may be the last book that I ever write, although I very much hope not. As long as I can type, I will fight and carry on regardless. As long as I can hear God telling me what to write, I will publish books and share His message with the world.

I do hope that this book and my story will help you realise that God still wants to use you. The question is, do you want to be used by God? Do you want to be part of what He is doing? Do you want to fight, overcome and witness the breakthrough in your own life?

I'm Still Valued

During the time that it has taken to write this

book, I have experienced three major visits to the hospital *(see timeline at the start)*. I remember not wanting to give up, with an, 'I've started so I'll finish' attitude, but it has taken a lot of effort. I even wrote some of it whilst in one of my hospital beds. I always grapple with how much to put in and how much to leave out. I decided to keep the chapters intentionally short but hopefully with enough information. My endeavours are mainly in the hope that you might be prompted to think about your own lives and your own problems which you may be facing in your own situations.

This is my continuing life story. The story has already unfolded and I feel it is only right to commit it to paper *(or Kindle if that is your thing)*.

For many months before even starting to write this book I was putting off writing it. I delayed by using an assortment of very good and genuine excuses to myself, I now understand why I hesitated on this project.

The title, 'I'm Still Valued', is what I honestly felt God wanted me to call this book, but there lies the problem. Do I believe this? Am I really still valued? Can I write this book with the honesty that it requires and needs? I feel that I have to if I want to maintain my integrity. However, in doing so, I will reveal my insecurities, talk about my fears and reveal my weaknesses. I will scrutinise myself and could easily pass a sentence of self-condemnation. The question rattles around in my head again; with all that I have wrong, physically, mentally and spiritually, how can God still value me? These are the thoughts that haunt me.

Am I alone in feeling this way? Do you ever question your worth, your purpose and your value? Of course you do *(if you're honest)*. Do you believe that God can and will still use you, even in your brokenness? Maybe you feel that you are simply too old and you want to be left to wait out your last days in heaven's waiting room. Perhaps you have been hurt by someone and you feel your confidence has gone, never to return. Do you compare yourself to others, and then condemn yourself as being inadequate and not good enough? This is called, 'Imposter Syndrome' and it is a lie. I now believe that even if you have one foot in the grave, God can still use you. I am an example of this and I hope that you will be encouraged by the stories that I now share with you.

*****

During a recent church meeting, we were asked to discuss John 14:9 when Jesus said, **"Because I live, you will live also."** We were asked the question, what does this statement mean to us? During the conversation, I realised that for me to live like Jesus, means to make a difference, change lives and have a purpose that leaves a positive impact. We can all do this in different ways, to various degrees and levels. We just have to make ourselves available to be used.

As mentioned, since I published my first book, my health has deteriorated, but I have also published thirteen more books including this one. In fact, I have been far more creative in the last nine years, than prior to my health issues. It would be so easy to say, "I am creative despite my health conditions", though I never say that. What I do say is that "I am even more creative, 'BECAUSE' of my physical limitations."

So, if you are wallowing in self-pity, self-condemnation and biding your time in 'heaven's waiting room', just STOP. You have a purpose and it is BECAUSE of your limitations and weaknesses that God can still use you. YOU ARE STILL VALUED. Do you believe that?

As I begin to share my continuing journey of this thing that we call life, I hope and pray that you will start to realise that, although bad things happen, good can come from them, if we allow it. I know that this story, in parts, will be difficult to convey. Maybe that is why I have been delaying writing it. Now though, I am reminded of another Bible verse.

'All things work together for the good
of those that are in Jesus Christ'
Romans 8:28

I am aware that some Christians often throw this verse around in a glib and trite fashion, but it is scripture, therefore, it must be true. Yet, we often fail to see the good or potential in a catastrophic event. Why should we? It is never easy to see the positive side of a negative situation. We easily blame God in our limited human nature. The problem is, that we look at situations and judge things with our 'human lens', whereas, we need to learn to see things through God's lens. When you start to do that, then you will know that 'you are still valued.' I will keep reminding you of this throughout this book.

*****

I briefly mentioned earlier that you may have been hurt by someone and you feel your confidence has gone, never to return. Why is it that some people have an innate ability to crush the dreams and potential of others? They make throwaway comments that damage a person's self-belief, confidence and emotional well-being. These people are rarely, actively aggressive and do not necessarily, intentionally set out to cause harm. They are subtle and passive in their aggression, gently eroding, wearing away and grinding down. We call such people, 'Toxic, Corrosive and Poisonous.' Do these labels make us feel better? No, of course not.

Have you encountered such people? Have you been a victim of such emotional abuse? Have you witnessed others subjected to this type of damaging treatment? It happens in families, throughout society, at your place of work and yes, even in the church.

I want to tell my story of how I encountered this, but in doing so, I realise that there is a potential to become like one of these people. So, I will be honest and speak with integrity, whilst purposefully avoiding mentioning any names of offenders, places or organisations.

I know that this kind of abusive behaviour is all around us and that people are afraid to speak out about it, especially in the Church and Christian organisations. However, it is only when someone speaks out that other victims can start to feel less isolated. They too may be encouraged to open up and share the pain that they have been through, or indeed are still going through.

The title of this book is, 'I'm Still Valued' and the truth is, we have always been valued by our Father God. Age, health, education, history, family, etc make no difference whatsoever. Disabilities, inabilities, capabilities and competence are still no barrier. You have always been valued by God.

This is my story of how God revealed this to me. This is the true story of God's continuing Golden Thread in my life, the hurdles that I have faced and continue to face and how God told me, I'm Still Valued.

Consider this...

1. Think about what Jesus said, "Because I live, you will live also." What does this statement mean to you?

2. How can you make yourself available to be used by God?

3. Has anyone ever spoken negative words over you, telling you that you are no good at something and that you should give up?

   How did you feel?

   What did you do?

Chapter Two
Tough Decision

I'm sure you've all heard the phrase '*When one door closes, another opens,*' because it's fairly common. However, during the process of change, an element of stress is usually hovering around. None of us enjoys being uncomfortable, least of all enduring any level of pain, for any great length of time. Yet despite this, it's surprising how much we can withstand. The kind of trauma that I am referring to in this chapter is emotional and mental pain. As a founder of The Door Youth Project, having worked tirelessly to develop it, the wrench of leaving was immense; far more than I could ever have imagined. To simply say that it was emotional, would be an understatement. My feelings were mixed with sorrow and joy.

I knew that if I remained as the Chief Executive Officer at The Door, I would eventually become a liability. I had been diagnosed with chronic kidney failure. I had known since 2008 about my Polycystic Kidney Disease and watched with concern as my kidney function dropped gradually. I knew that at some point in the future, in order to stay alive, I would require dialysis. By September 2012, just four years after diagnosis, my kidney function had already dropped to just above 30%. I was then in stage 3b kidney failure and by the time I stepped down from The Door Youth Project, in November 2014, I was already at 21% *(stage 4)*.

At this point, I had better explain something. Kidney failure has five different stages, with stage five also being referred to as '*End-Stage.*' Each phase brings with it a new set of symptoms or increasing severity of the existing ones. At stage 3b I mainly had high blood pressure, which was controlled by medication, but the realist in me knew that the next step was only round the corner.

Now, if you are thinking that this is going to be a story of miraculous healing and that my kidney function will be restored, then you are in for a disappointing read. I did receive an abundance of prayer, but still, my kidney function declined. I know that God could physically heal me if it was His will, but He didn't. However, even though we may not experience physical healing, healing can still come in many forms. We worship 'Jehovah Rapha' – God who heals. I do say that I have received healing, it is an inner healing and I will explain how later.

I wanted to do the best thing for The Door Youth Project, so in 2012, decided to work on a two-year exit strategy. I informed the Chair of the Trustees and a few of the senior management team. The Chair didn't want to accept it. He couldn't understand. Why should he? He saw a fit, healthy, competent and rising leader. He asked me to reconsider and to give it a year before making a final decision, to which I agreed, although the senior management team already knew what my answer would be. I did it in this way, partly for my own mind, which would have to come to terms with the decision. In 2012 I had been there for 22 years and my mum, who had the same kidney disease as me, had only recently died. I was therefore, dealing with grief on multiple levels. I also did it for the sake of the organisation. Part of my role included all of the fundraising and income generation, so I would work diligently, with enthusiasm to train a young apprentice as a Fundraiser, whilst hoping there was a good amount of funding by the time I left. Little did I know at the time, that the apprentice, would be a kind of lifesaver to me during those final two years. As I worked alongside him, teaching him, I still felt valued.

Consider this...

1. What major changes have you struggled with in your life?

2. How did they make you feel?

3. Have you made any regrettable decisions as a result of change?

Chapter Three
Not the man I used to be?

During those last two years at The Door, it was more than my physical health that eroded, my mental well-being also deteriorated, though, as the Chief Executive, I had to visually keep it together. I believed at the time, that as the leader, the person at the top, I had to stay strong and try not to show any signs of weakness. I thought that, if I admitted I was struggling with depression and anxiety, it would be a mistake. Implementation of change in any organisation is a delicate process and the bigger the change, the more sensitive preparations and procedures need to be. As I look back now, I wonder if I lacked some wisdom. Did I fail to understand how this huge change might impact others? During these last two years, there was a noticeable shift in the atmosphere. Where there was once peace, there was now tension, uncertainty and anxiety. It was noticeable in me and in others.

I was struggling and because of that, failed to acknowledge others may be feeling the same or even worse. During that last year, some of the staff would question me about why I wanted to leave, and this only made the struggle harder, as I didn't '*want*' to leave, I had to leave, and I felt as if I didn't really have a choice. I tried to explain about my deteriorating health conditions, though I am sure some of them thought that I was being melodramatic.

Others, it seemed, were more impatient and frustrations started to show in their behaviour and words. At times it felt as if they couldn't wait to be rid of me. I may have been completely wrong in my feelings, as self-doubt and imposter syndrome started to take hold. I felt like a washed-up, unwanted, good-for-nothing, 'has-been'.

I looked for God's strength to carry me. I remembered the Bible verse, '*The joy of the Lord is my strength*' *(Nehemiah 8:10b)*, but struggled to find any joy in what I was doing. Then my young apprentice would ask a question, I would explain and he would learn; I felt useful again. I drew strength from those moments of joy and wondered, is this joy from the Lord?

During those last two years as the CEO, I had so many questions and doubts. Was I doing the right thing? What did my future hold? Would anyone ever want me to work for them? I felt worthless, lost and confused. I had a fear of not being good enough and I knew that that fear could lead me to a place of not being able to live with myself; I had been there before.

Three curses

Where do those negative feelings come from? They don't just happen overnight; they slowly build as the seeds of doubt are planted in your mind. The words that are spoken over us can give birth to a decline in self-worth and without awareness you are no longer the person that you used to be.

A single, offhand, throwaway remark can cause so much damage. I would even go as far as to say, it can leave you cursed. I will quickly add that I have now learned not to accept these types of comments. I do seriously regard them as a curse and I now know that a curse can have no hold on you if you reject it.

I have struggled with my decision to share these stories but I also feel, that to leave out this part of my journey of pain, would be incomplete. It is also the foundation of the grief and pain that would come.

The first curse was placed on me in September 2012. I was reflectively thinking about my future and what God would have me do next and during a conversation with a friend, I mentioned that I might write a book. My mum had inspired me to think this, as when she died, we found the start of a story about her life. Although she never finished it, it was enough to plant a seed, the thought of, *'I could do that.'*

So, I vocalised my thoughts and the conversation went like this. "I'm thinking of becoming an author."

The response somewhat surprised me, "You couldn't possibly be an author", I respected this person's opinion so I asked, "Oh, why not?"

"Because authors write 3,600 words in an hour and you could never do that."

It was said with such authority, confidence and knowledge that I just accepted it. "You're right, I could never do that." I thought that my crippled finger would always slow me down, but I now know that no disability should EVER stop anyone from following a dream. This one throwaway comment would delay my writing like a curse. God was speaking to me, leading me, but a massive barrier had just been built and it would hold me back for years.

Almost two years later, in the summer of 2014, I pushed that barrier out of the way and I wrote my first book, my biographical story called, 'The Golden Thread'. It was published over a year later after a Kickstarter funding campaign. It felt good to have a book published and even better knowing that other people had helped to make it possible, they believed in me. I have learnt a great deal more about publishing since that first book.

I also knew that my story could impact the lives of many and to share it was a way of glorifying God. Incidentally, that book is still being read all over the world and I often hear from someone whose life was changed through reading it. Back then though, in 2015, I still struggled to consider myself an author, with the comment still echoing in my mind, *"You could never be an author."*

In agreement, I found myself thinking, "Yeah,

it's a one-off, a fluke, anyone can write ONE book. It doesn't make you an author." – Imposter Syndrome continued to take hold.

That then was that decision made, I'm not an author and it's time to move on. Yet, God is patient and He had other plans, it would take another three years before I knew exactly what He would require of me, but I'll tell you about that later.

*****

I can't remember the exact time the second curse was placed on me, but it was in 2014 *(my final year)*. I developed The Door Youth Project after being employed as the first paid worker in 1996. Over an eighteen-year period, I raised the profile of the organisation, raised awareness of the community and had proven my skills in marketing, communication and public relations – skills that God has given me.

Now that I have set the scene and the background, try to imagine how I felt to hear someone say, "The Door needs to find someone to help with marketing, as they're not very good at it." They were right, as any organisation, no matter who they are, could do with some extra help when it comes to marketing and communications. The way that it was said though was cold and blunt, it felt personal.

Ouch! I felt that and it hurt. The wound went deep and more imposter syndrome seeds were planted. "Maybe they are right", I thought.

> *"People will forget what you said,*
> *people will forget what you did,*
> *but people will never forget*
> *how you made them feel."*
> *Maya Angelou*

Six years later, I decided to wipe away that thought and doubt. So, in 2020, I studied for a level 5 advanced diploma in digital marketing. I passed every assignment with distinction and completed the whole course in a few short months, it should have taken two years.

The person who had made the original comment, had not been aware of the mental damage caused by one single, flippant remark, but the curse had been lifted. Although they were none the wiser, I felt a small victory and knew that the skills that God had given me had made this possible and I am now professionally providing this service for others.

*****

The third big attack on my abilities was aimed at my skill as a Youth Worker, so it cut to the core of what God had called me to do. As the time for my departure from The Door approached, I received an enquiry from a local Parish Council, they were seeking professional advice on how to inject new life into their failing youth club in the village.

During a meeting with the councillors, one of them voiced his opinion. "Ideally, we would like Brendan to come along and sort us out."

I felt honoured that they would specifically want me, as this was the youth club that I had grown up in. At the age of 16 years old, I was the Chair of the junior committee, so it meant a great deal to me.

Before I had a chance to answer, someone interjected, "You don't want Brendan, he's been out of frontline youth work for five years." They implied that I was a 'has-been.' I felt small and crushed.

It was a lie, but a convincing lie. For a moment, it even convinced me. Then, I started to think about the comment. I had not worked in general youth work for three years, but during all of that time, I had always been involved in some form of youth specialism. Once again, I felt belittled and worthless, my self-belief diminished and imposter syndrome cast a shadow over my life again.

This curse was broken within a few months when the same Parish Councillor contacted me. He had heard that I was leaving The Door and was planning to help small charities as a freelance consultant. The local village youth club became one of my first clients and with a year-long contract, I was able to inject new life, new funding and save it from closure. For me, it lifted my soul and gave me a new sense of belonging, and a purpose; it made me feel valued again.

Ironically, it was a secular organisation that now filled me with worth. As for my ability to work with young people, I ran four different youth clubs and the young people loved it – they loved me – God was still using and leading me – another curse had been broken.

This village and the youth club were the first of

many to benefit from my consultancy, but it was symbiotic, as I also started to realise just how much knowledge I had and I wanted to share every ounce of that knowledge.

I'll end this section with a short story about how I introduced the youth club and the young people to transformational youth work and in particular, restorative justice.

In readiness to reopen the centre, a group of volunteers had been decorating and clearing out decades' worth of accumulated junk. A skip had been filled and now sat on the tarmac driveway. Job well done.

That evening, a group of bored teenagers were hanging around outside the club, they felt that it was their space, even though it had been closed for a year. They pulled wooden boards from the skip and made makeshift skateboard ramps, then they found the old tins of paint. After a little honest tomfoolery, Chris (not his real name) threw a can of paint into the air. On impact with the tarmac, it exploded like a giant red paint bomb.

The CCTV system replayed all of this and the

management team insisted that the Police be involved. I agreed, although they also wanted Chris banned and charged. It took a lot for me to convince them to try a new way. I was pleased to see the local police officer arrive. I had known PC Lizzie Brown *(not her real name),* for many years and I knew that she would be an advocate of restorative justice. I knew that she was a Christian, so for me, it was an added bonus. The Council listened to her and allowed us to deal with the issue however we felt best.

We let it be known to a few young people that we knew it was Chris and that we wanted to chat with him. It didn't take long, as Chris turned up at the centre shortly afterwards. He was petrified, afraid that he was going to be arrested. Word had also spread about police involvement. He genuinely apologised and asked what he could do to make things right. Whilst we were chatting, his friend filled a bucket with water and grabbed a brush from the kitchen. Chris turned from me and started to scrub with desperation, but the water was cold and the paint was gloss. It had dried in two days.

I boiled kettles of hot water and poured them on as he scrubbed and his friends all gathered in a circle, watching but not helping. Then Alex piped up and said that his dad had a jet washer that we could use. He ran home and returned five minutes later. Eventually, a whole team of young people came to help Chris and the paint was all removed.

PC Lizzie did visit Chris's home and chatted with his parents. I was present as extra support for Chris and that was the end of the situation. A few weeks later, Chris came to see me and thanked me. He told me that it was the wake-up call that he needed, that he had been doing a lot of silly things and that it could have been a lot worse. Restorative justice had worked. I'm not sure what happened to Chris after that, but hopefully, nothing that involved breaking the law. For me, the whole incident confirmed that I was still a great youth worker and that I was still valued.

Consider this…

1. Do you notice shifts in the atmosphere?

   What does this look like?

2. When have you been challenged about a decision made?

    How did you feel?

    What did you learn?

3. What Bible verse can you stand on for comfort and strength?

Chapter Four
More pain

In February 2014, whilst still working at The Door, I felt under immense pressure with increasing anxiety. The uncertainty of where the money was coming from, the demands of managing staff in a growing organisation, together with the challenges of working with young people with their own problems. The personal burdens regarding the future; my future and that of the project were all stacking up.

The mental strain developed into physical symptoms. I was waking up in the morning with serious chest pain. Six years earlier, in the same year that I was diagnosed with kidney disease, I was also told that I had angina *(narrowing of the arteries)*. It had been stable until now, but due to the unpredictable nature of change, my condition was becoming unstable. As a result, I was rushed to the hospital and fitted with my first three coronary stents. Not for one moment did I even consider this health issue was stress related, but I do now. On reflection, I can see that for this reason alone, leaving the project was the right decision.

On 3rd November 2014, I eventually left The Door Youth Project. People would ask me if I missed being there and I would always say, "No." I had given myself two years to mentally prepare and at first, everything felt fine. I had the new challenge of a failing youth centre to focus on, which I believe God provided for me.

If I missed anything, it was the young people and staff whom I had built close relationships with. I didn't miss the stress, the struggles and the daily grind *(some weeks I had worked 60 to 70 hours)*. I didn't miss the monitoring, budgets or fundraising and I certainly didn't miss the responsibility.

To be honest, it was a relief to be free. Don't get me wrong, I had an enjoyable time at The Door, it was such a fun place to work and so rewarding to see the positive changes in so many young people. I hold on tight to the good years and try to forget the cost and the toll that some periods had on my life.

To make matters worse, *(but again without going into too much detail)*, soon after leaving The Door, we *(my wife Heather and I)*, withdrew from all church life and local churches. We rarely ventured out as we struggled to be in the company of any other people.

This only left me feeling let down, alone, broken, angry and bitter. The Door and the church had been my life and support network until those last two years of confusion and pain. I didn't realise it at the time but I was grieving. I tried to deny my loss but my feelings morphed into anger and bitterness which festered into the most painful of wounds. We did have a few close Christian friends who understood and tried to help, but healing could not be forced, it takes time. The pain was growing into agony and I was spiritually dying, like the walking wounded. Although the scars were invisible, at times the symptoms of mental illness were very visible.

Occasionally someone would ask what church I go to. I would respond with the rather cynical answer, "The worldwide church of broken Christians – it's the biggest church in the world."

At the time that is how it felt and how my feelings manifested. I would meet other Christians *(mainly online)* who had been hurt by fellow Christians – friendly fire. I wandered that barren place of the outcast for almost a year, with the bitterness propagating within. Then, a close Christian friend guided us toward a small group of Christians who met weekly in a home. The group was led by a local Christian and everyone in the group accepted us warmly and in love. Only one person in the group knew me and my history and she was glad to see me there. It was just what I needed for a short season and the comfort of peer support started me on a journey of restoration.

In my darkest moments of frustration, God would pour poetry into me. He had given me the gift of rhyme in my first year of inviting Him into my life. I sensed a strong connection to Him as He spoke the words into my heart.

The poems were a form of release, but they also indicated to me that I was still in pain... like this one for example.

Let it Drop

Why do I keep letting people under my skin?
Not recognising, that in doing so, they win?
Why do I allow the scoffers so much credit?

When I know that deep down inside,
I need to just forget it?
You see it's so easy to say
"forgive and forget."
Yet oh!
The pain and the hurt won't let go.
Constant reminders,
memories and flashbacks.
Cutting like a knife,
slash, slash, slash hack.
Can't let go, won't let go, don't know.
How to? What's true? Do you?
Do you?
You and your lies, they get under my skin!
You and your lies, I let them win!
Why, oh why, oh why, oh why?
It doesn't have to be like this?
I cry, I cry, I cry, I cry?
And you just take the - please stop.
Please make it stop!
Please, please, will you please just
let it drop?

Consider this...

1. After change, how did God provide for
   you?

Did you even notice?

2. What changes have happened in your life
    that you had no control over?

3. Have you ever felt worthless and devalued
    by others, especially those who you regard
    as friends?

4. Where can you find the right help?

    Who can you share your struggles with?

5. Can you think about your own creative
    skills and start to use them in a
    therapeutic way? – Try writing poetry.

Chapter Five
Moving on

A year after leaving The Door, my time at the now thriving local youth centre was coming to an end. I had no intention of staying longer than the year, even though the young people and the staff asked me not to leave. I had managed to hide my health issues, it was easier then, but in the end, I had to explain. "I have kidney failure and I need to leave because I don't want to become a liability. I could soon be in need of dialysis and at some point, will need a transplant. I've done what I came here to do."

At that time in my life, specifically September 2015, those words of 'dialysis' and 'transplant' were only words. The same remote, 2nd hand concept, just as they seem to anyone who has never encountered what they actually are. However, I would have a far greater understanding during the year to come.

By February 2016, my kidney function had fallen to 15% and I was now in '*end stage*' kidney failure. It sounded final like the end was nigh, but... there was still an epic journey to travel. In that same month, I was assessed as suitable for a transplant and my name was added to the waiting list. That list contained at least another 5,000 other people in the UK. This thought was daunting and I tried hard to imagine what 5,000 people would look like. All that I could think was, *'Well, that is a lot.'* I started to ponder, more and more. What if they all needed a transplant more than me? They surely had more worth and value than me. Even when my health was deteriorating and my life was at risk, I downplayed it and did not consider myself worthy of another person's kidney. God did though.

My symptoms were now more obvious, so, I did pray that a suitable donor would be found soon. I guess in God's eyes, *'soon'* could be years. Turns out it absolutely was. Little did I know that I would in fact, have to wait another three years before I would receive a transplant. The waiting game began, so I took one day at a time, never knowing when I might receive the call, with much of my life on hold. I'll explain more about this later.

Looking back, I now realise that this is where my feeling that God had abandoned me started. I didn't vocalise it, because I hadn't thought about it, but I did feel alone, looking towards an unknown future. It would take me over two years before I finally voiced my feelings, two years before I was so broken and God would speak into my darkness.

I never stopped praying but I did give up on asking others to pray for me. For years I had received prayer for my kidney disease and I gradually came to a place of acceptance. I know that nothing is impossible for God, so that means it is well within His abilities to heal me but for whatever reason, He chose not to.

I think the final turning point of waiting for that healing came one evening when I attended a Christian event. A well-known speaker with a healing ministry would be preaching. Before going, I prayed and asked God to give the speaker or someone else a word of knowledge about someone with kidney problems. After the sermon, the preacher had several words of knowledge for other people. He prayed for people with various pains and conditions but he never once asked if there was anyone present in need of prayer for a kidney problem and nobody else had a word.

The evening was coming to a close and I was at a place of acceptance and just about to leave. At that point, two ladies who were known to me and knew of my illness asked if I would like to receive prayer. It tried to explain that I didn't want any prayer and that I was okay. The conversation lasted several minutes as they tried to convince me, whilst all the time I declined their prayer. Then the unbelievable happened, they prayed anyway.

I sat there, stunned at first, unable to say anything to stop them. As they continued to pray my feeling of shock turned into disgust and I was fuming with anger. When they had both finished their onslaught, I looked at them both and told them, "I didn't ask for prayer, I asked you not to do that. Now I feel as if I have been spiritually raped."

I learned a lot that evening about listening to what people tell you, to respect their wishes and who they are. I grasped never to force your own agenda onto anyone. I hope that the two well-meaning ladies also learnt the same.

*****

For work, I scraped by with a little bit of charity consulting work, but it wasn't enough to live off. Heather wasn't working and so we survived using our savings, *(or rather a small inheritance that we had been given).* We had hoped that it would help us during our retirement, but we needed it now.

We can often fail to notice the small steps that God provides for us, which can lead us to something bigger. One such step for me was to start working with a local infant bereavement charity. I spent several months helping them to develop and find the funding that they needed to expand. Eventually, I helped them to recruit someone to replace me. Once again, I didn't want to become a liability. When it was time to hand over and leave, the Chair of the Trustees thanked me. It was a sincere, heartfelt thank you. She went further and explained that I had saved her charity from closure. I had shown them what they could do and given them hope.

They had also given me something.

It was during one of the fund applications that the funding source asked for a short video about the charity. I made that film using my phone and a very basic editing programme. Little did I know that this was the start of a whole new level of creativity that was going to grow out of my adversity. This one, very basic film, would lead me to create hundreds of films under the banner of Message Movies.

In the Bible, we read that the Apostle Paul was a tent maker and he made tents to provide an income to support his ministry. Film production and digital marketing are now my equivalent to Paul's tent-making. It brings in some money, although not much and it also allows me time and space for my own creative ministry.

A different kind of hospital

We knew we had to find a church that we could feel comfortable in. It would not be easy, because I was so well-known among the local churches. We considered going further afield, to a place where no one knew anything about us, but that was not the answer.

So, in June 2016, we walked into the Five Valleys Christian Fellowship. We were made to feel extremely welcome. It was a warm, genuine reception, with no questions asked. It is so important to welcome people in the best way for them. This takes discernment by the Holy Spirit, sensitivity and acceptance through grace and love. We were searching and were allowed the space to investigate, without any perceived threats. We were also listened to which was just what we needed.

Five Valleys Christian Fellowship did all this and nobody seemed shocked to see us. Nobody questioned our motives for being there and there were so many friendly faces.

We were spiritually injured, victims of Christian friendly fire, the walking wounded and we had just walked into a hospital. We had taken the first step on the road to recovery, but the journey would be long. We are still on it and we always will be.

Although we were new to the church and hadn't really committed to it, we were invited to attend their summer camp. It was a small gathering at the Lenchwood Christian Centre and we went along with our motorhome. It was here that we really started to get to know people more. I was invited to play in the worship team and to share a short testimony. For the first time in nearly two years, I began to feel valued again *(in a Christian context)*.

> *"For where two or three are gathered together in my name, there am I in the midst of them."*
> Matt. 18:19–20

Even though it was just a small gathering, the Holy Spirit turned up and ministered to us all. It was a powerful presence. During the third evening, I was playing with the band, the meeting had progressed into a time of ministry as many were stepping forward for prayer.

I sensed the Holy Spirit nudging me, convicting me to ask for prayer myself. I ignored the nudge but I started to feel warmer as the Holy Spirit continued to touch me. I still didn't move, I carried on playing whilst something was welling up inside of me. My heart beat was fast. It was uncomfortable, almost painful like something was trying to burst out.

Let me pause this story for a moment while I add some background scenery.

I had recently read RT Kendal's book entitled, 'Total Forgiveness' *(which I highly recommend)*. I discovered what forgiveness actually is and crucially, what unforgiveness really looks like. A valuable lesson or insight had been revealed to me. For example, I realised that simply holding a grudge against a person over something can rot and fester inside of us. If not dealt with, this can grow into feelings of resentment, so you can become angry, which then can present itself as hostile thoughts towards them. Although the incident itself may have been quite minor, it manifests in bitterness and can build into what seems like a crime against humanity to you!

It can get very personal indeed. You can also start to feel that same animosity towards others, who appear friendly towards the original perpetrator. Although they had nothing whatsoever to do with what happened, they become guilty simply by association. It's usually those friends who you perceive to have absolutely no problem with your nemesis. It's especially annoying if you've shared deeply personal thoughts with them, highlighting your concerns. You can even start blaming them because it can appear like they actively encourage your enemy's behaviour. It seems as if these trusted friends just don't understand how you've arrived at these conclusions and why it has become so important to you. It's very easy to retreat from those relationships as well because it's like they have dismissed you, ignoring the situation entirely. It's almost as if they don't even believe you anymore and now, they're batting for the other side entirely!

You can see how these situations can get completely out of hand. The hurting individual can lose most of their perspective. Ultimately unforgiveness doesn't stop growing as it begins to destroy you.

I was now so overwhelmed with this manifestation of bitterness and a battle was taking place within my heart. It was spiritual, but the spiritual state had become a physical one.

So, back to the events unfolding at camp.

I left the stage with tears trickling down my cheeks. The unburdening had already emerged, although there was much more to come. I briefly explained to people around me that I needed prayer for unforgiveness, so two people prayed for me. Then the taps really opened. Tears poured down my face and I don't exaggerate when I say, I was soaked. I released the names of those whom I had harboured resentment against. One by one, I named them quietly so that no one else could hear.

The release was instantaneous. My chest stopped banging and I cooled down. The power of unforgiveness had held me in captivity for nearly two years, yet the power of forgiveness gave me unbridled freedom right where I stood.

Forgiveness, however, for human beings, is an ongoing process. Our mind can continue to hold us back as we don't forget, so I do still find that I have to continue to forgive. This may sound odd to some people. Surely if God sets you free, you are set free? Yes, that is true, I was set free from the bitterness of unforgiveness and I don't want that to creep back in again. That is why I continue to forgive.

I often wonder what kind of mess I would be in now if I hadn't been brought to that place of forgiveness. It was like the end of a battle and as usual, God's timing was perfect, as I prepared for my next battle. This one would be physical.

Consider this...

1. Are you holding on to unforgiveness?

   Has it developed into bitterness?

   Are you ready to forgive? Find someone to pray with you.

2. Have you considered volunteering your valuable skills to an organisation in need?

3. As we find hope, we can see fear diminish – Where do you find the hope that you need?

4. Make a list of the ways that you do or can help others – including even the smallest things.

5. When you have helped others, how did it make you feel?

6. Where can you find fellowship and support with like-minded Christians?

Chapter Six
I will survive (dialysis)

The church camp ended on Friday 11th August 2016 and just four days later on the 15th, I was in the hospital for surgery. It was *'elective'* surgery, meaning that I had chosen this and that I knew that it was coming. Really? I didn't choose renal failure. I didn't choose dialysis, but it was a necessary means to stay alive. I certainly didn't choose any of the impediments that my body would experience, least of all a complication that could end my life.

When I told a close friend that I was thinking of writing this book, I mentioned that I wasn't sure about talking about the sordid details relating to my medical conditions. He scoffed at me saying, "You have to put it all in and make it real, don't sanitise it." So, this is real, it's what happened. It was horrible, but God was walking through it with me.

My kidney function remained at 15% for 6 months and so toxins had begun to build up in my body. I now had several, noticeable *(to me, but invisible to most)*, daily symptoms. I had an almost constant headache, together with nausea and increasing fatigue. My urine output reduced, causing my body to retain fluid and I started to vomit on occasions. I knew that I needed dialysis if I was going to survive and I was given a choice of HD or PD.

The most common form of dialysis is HD – Haemodialysis. This method involves surgery to create a fistula in your arm, which is simply an easy entry point. You then go to the hospital three times every week to be piped up to a machine. Blood is pumped out of you via the fistula, cleaned by the machine and then pumped back into your body. I didn't like the sound of so many trips to the hospital and nearly half of your week destroyed, so I opted for PD instead.

Peritoneal dialysis has its own negative issues that I was not really aware of, but I would soon find out. This next part is all sciencey, so please bear with me. The peritoneum is a membrane that lines the inside of your abdomen and pelvis *(parietal layer)*. It also covers many of your organs inside *(visceral layer)*. The space in between these layers is called your peritoneal cavity. For PD the cavity is filled with a glucose solution, which is a thick solution. Through the process of osmosis *(remember school science)* the thinner solution or fluids that are held in your body can pass into the thicker solution. Then at the appropriate time, the waste fluid is drained off and replaced with a new glucose solution. PD patients have another choice, manual draining or using a machine. At first, you have to use the manual method and drain the fluid off at least three times each day. That, to me, was too much of the day wasted, so I would opt for the machine, but first, a catheter *(a flexible pipe)* needed to be inserted into my abdomen.

So, here I was in this elective surgery.

The whole procedure was considered quick and simple. It was scheduled as day surgery, so I would be home and in my own bed that night – or so I thought.

The surgery went according to plan and I was back on the day ward just after lunch. I managed to force down a slice of toast and then they asked me to drink a litre of water. I needed to be able to pee before they would allow me to leave to go home. I couldn't go, so I drank some more and then even more.

Although the human bladder does have a potentially large capacity and is able to stretch, just like a balloon, there comes a point of bursting. Unable to pee, I reached that point and was in agony. The nurses decided to scan my bladder, but the day ward didn't have a scanner. I waited in excruciating pain for well over an hour whilst they searched the hospital for a scanner.

I kept screaming at them to find a scanner, I told them that I thought I was about to burst. The pain really was unbelievable. I also knew enough about human anatomy to deduce that the ONLY way my bladder would empty and the pain subside, was to insert a urinary tract catheter. Although I had never before experienced this procedure, I sensed that it would not be pleasant, but something needed to be done quickly.

Have you ever heard the expression, *'Sometimes we need to go through more pain to find relief'?* In this case, this statement was very true, though I was not aware of the extent of pain and suffering my body was about to undergo.

When we reach a certain pain threshold or a certain state desperation, any dignity is cast aside and you just let the medical team do what they have to. I know that the two nurses were gentle as they thrust the pipe into my penis, but the pain was torture and I screamed loud. I could hear the other patients make concerned comments. It seemed to last forever. As it broke through the sphincter muscle, I felt immediate relief and urine began to flow. Within a few minutes, 3.3 litres filled the container at the end of the plastic tube. I felt relieved, that I had been relieved. The current threat had been averted or so we thought. The bladder problem was simply an early sign of something even more sinister that was happening in my body.

Heather came to collect me and I was discharged around 6.00 pm, with the catheter still in place and a bag strapped to my leg. She pushed me down to the car in a wheelchair, but as I stood to move into the car, I told her that I didn't feel very well.

I deteriorated more during the half-hour journey and decided to go straight to bed. By 7.00 pm my head was in a bowl and black vomit poured out of me. I have heard many people joke that, no matter what you have eaten, vomit always looks like you have eaten carrots. This didn't, it was just like coffee grounds and it kept coming, there was so much of it; far more than any stomach could hold. It was frightening.

Heather called for an ambulance and I found myself back in the hospital by 8.00 pm. The accident and emergency department was busy and no one was telling me much. Slowly the coffee grounds stopped and turned into a thick, black, sticky liquid. It tasted disgusting.

A doctor arrived to insert a nasal gastric tube *(NG tube)*. The tube was forced up my nose, down my throat and into my stomach. I was given some water to swallow, to make to tube go down easier, but it was so difficult. With the tube in place, they attached a syringe and gradually sucked liquid from my stomach. The tube was then attached to a clear plastic bag and slowly the offending black liquid was syphoned into the bag. That tube would remain in place for the next three days.

A CT scan was deemed necessary to determine the cause of the problem. Was there a blockage? As I lay on the bed of the scanner, I threw up even more black liquid. This was the point that fear hit me and I asked the nurse, "What is that stuff?"

She simply said, "That is what is inside of you. You are very ill."

Talk about stating the obvious, but just the tone and calmness of her voice were enough to settle my nerves.

It would be another three days and I would spend time in two different wards before I would finally find myself in a side room of the renal ward. That was when I was told that I had experienced a paralytic ileus. All that they told me was that it was a very serious condition, so I consulted Google and found out, it is a condition where the motor activity of the bowel is impaired; it went into spasm. The black vomit was the contents of my bowel being forced backwards. Google also told me that it is serious and if prolonged and untreated will result in death.

So, August 2016 was the first time that I had such a close brush with death. I thanked God that I was still alive and asked Him to forgive me for being so afraid. It was very scary, remember I had a tube in my abdomen, one up my willie and another up my nose and my insides pouring out of my mouth. How would you react?

I had faced death and beat it, but I had no concept, that I would face more deeply miserable and terrifying trauma again and again during the next seven years and that hospital would become like a second home.

Consider this…

1. As you have become older, there may be things that you can no longer do. Try to focus on the positive things and make a list of what you can do, be sure to include all the new things that you are going to try.

2. Try to reflect on the fact that there is always someone in a much worse state than you are and keep smiling.

3. If you know someone with serious health issues and struggles, what can you do to help them?

Chapter Seven
Will I survive (dialysis)?

I called the previous chapter, *'I Will Survive'* as I had conquered death. Why then, do I suddenly switch the words in that title to, *'Will I Survive?"*

After one event we move on to the next. That is life. I now had to grasp the reality of peritoneal dialysis and at first, it was overwhelming, with so much to take in. By the way, the word *'overwhelming'* is an under-exaggeration and at first, I wondered if I would cope. Had I made the right decision?

Hygiene was the most important and the first thing that I had to learn, before even starting dialysis. Remember, the tube that exited my abdomen was in my Peritoneum and poor hygiene could result in Peritonitis, a very serious infection that, if untreated, could kill.

The initial problem is the amount of information that you have to learn. I believe that this hurdle is one of the reasons why most people opt for haemodialysis, which is mainly done for you by a nurse. PD is self-administered, which is why I chose it. I wondered if I would ever grasp all that I needed to learn, then one day, another PD patient, who was about a month ahead of me assured me. "You'll get there, it's hard at first, but it suddenly all makes sense."

He was right and a month later I started dialysis and made the same reassuring remarks to people just learning. At the start, I attended the hospital three times each week and that just robs you of life.

Another thing to get used to was the enormous mountain of boxes that were delivered every month to my home. These heavy boxes were full of fluid and equipment, enough to fill a pallet. Every month Heather tirelessly carried all of the boxes upstairs into a bedroom which was now a designated store room. The sheer sight of the boxes was daunting and a constant reminder of my condition. Of course, having a tube coming out of your abdomen and a belly full of fluid was also a reminder, but the colossal mountain triggered a negative feeling – DEPRESSION.

You may be thinking that I regret opting for PD and should have chosen HD. Don't get me wrong, I did make the right choice and the best choice for me, but renal failure is hard, whatever choices you make. You may also be wondering why I'm making such a big deal about starting dialysis and that maybe I have exaggerated the title of this chapter – *'Will I Survive?'*

Each of the previously mentioned issues were pretty lame in comparison to this next problem that I now experienced – *'Drain Pain.'*

When I used to make wine, I would syphon off the good clear wine and leave the dregs, the sediment in the bottom of the jar. You never wanted to suck up that sediment, that would be bad. When I had a fish tank and I had to clean it out, it was the opposite. I wanted to suck away at the bottom of the tank as to syphon off the dregs instead. I actually found it quite therapeutic. The final visual image that I will give you is that of drinking a milkshake through a straw. Who can resist sucking up that last little drop? Despite making that rude sound at the bottom, it really is worth it.

Peritoneal dialysis is very similar to these three examples. When I started to fill my abdomen with fluid, then at the appropriate time, transfer it back out of my body, I was surprised by the pain.

At first, I had to use the manual method whilst my body became used to it. This method relies on syphoning the fluid, so it is relatively gentle, that is until that tube starts to suck on the bottom. The tube lies low, deep within your pelvic region and as you would expect, there are numerous nerve endings throughout the lining. Just like that milkshake straw, the tube sucks to remove every last drop and as it sucks on a nerve end pain shoots through your body. I know that I am carrying two litres of fluid and that it has to come out, but the pain often started at the point of 1.5 litres, with another half a litre left to suck out. The pain increases as the fluid reduces.

At times the pain shoots sideways or straight up through my body, depending on which nerve has been aggravated. These pains are severe, however, by far the most painful and the most frequent are the times that the sucking tube makes contact in the lower pelvic region, where the nerve endings are also attached to my penis. I can only describe the pain as electrical charges to the end of my penis.

On a scale of ten with ten being the highest, these pains were bearable at about three to five and they would last up to 15 minutes. In the same way that sucking the last of a milkshake is worth it, I now told myself the same, *'It is worth it, it is worth it, it's better than being dead.'* This was a kind of mantra that I would repeat in my head, as I tried to remain positive.

Thirst also became another problem, as anyone who is on any form of dialysis knows, I was on a strict fluid restriction. Normal, healthy people are all told to drink plenty of fluids and I was used to drinking many litres of water every day. Keep your kidneys flushed, it's good for them, is the standard advice. So, a fluid restriction on any level is hard. My restriction was reasonable at 2 litres each day because I was still able to urinate a litre. I would suck on ice cubes and make my own ice lollies as a form of comfort to quench my thirst, but there was nothing that I could do to ease the drain pain.

After just two weeks on the manual drain, three times every day and finding it totally absorbing and time-consuming, I switched to the automatic option. This would release my days as I was connected to a machine every night for an eight-hour cycle. It would fill me and empty me as I slept, but first, the process started with the usual scrub-up, connect up and drain down. Instead of syphoning and using gravity, the machine pumped and it was aggressive.

My penis pain was unbearable and I would often be in tears with such excruciating torture. The pain now measured a maximum of 10 *(top of the scale)* and would last in excess of 15 minutes. I couldn't hold back the tears and the screams. I questioned if it was really worth it. Is it really worth making that rude and uncouth noise just for a few more drops of milkshake? Was it worth the agonising suffering, just to prolong life? What sort of life was this?

I developed a pain scale where I multiplied the pain level by the number of minutes of suffering. The resulting score was monitored on a spreadsheet and I created graphs. Some of the scores were over 200. It may sound like a crazy thing to do, but the nurses were impressed and it gave me some form of being in control, although I really was far from it.

I knew that one of my nurses was a Christian and although it was against all of the rules, I asked her to pray for me. She did and after that, things did start to improve slightly and slowly. You could argue that my body was just adjusting and becoming accustomed to the process, as it does, but I was so thankful for my prayer prescription.

I could already feel the physical pain starting to impact my mental health and I hadn't even been on dialysis for two months. I knew that mentally I could crash very quickly, so had to think of something fast. I needed to find a distraction, something creative and something that would make me feel valued.

Consider this...

1. What are you currently going through that seems overwhelming?

2. Who can you turn to for help?

   There is always someone.

3. How are you coping mentally?

   Be honest with yourself and care about yourself.

Chapter Eight
Dog fight or flight?

Just to remind you, I left The Door Youth Project on 3rd November 2014. I felt washed up, rejected and devalued. Then, exactly two years later on 3rd November 2016, I played my first gig with a band. This is that story and how I once again felt useful, wanted and valued.

*****

Some time ago at church, at the start of a new year, we were encouraged to seek God for one single word for the year. The word that came to my mind was tenacious and I had to look it up to see what it meant. This is what I read.

➢ Tending to keep a firm hold of something; clinging or adhering closely.

➢ Not readily relinquishing a position, principle, or course of action; determined.

➢ Persisting in existence; not easily dispelled.

I learnt to fight at an early age, it's in my nature not to give up, tenacious truly is my word. At first, when I was young, I used my fists. I ran toward trouble and never flew away from it. Later in life when I found Jesus or did He find me? I'm never quite sure about that, after all, I was lost and was in need of finding. Anyway, when my relationship with Jesus started, I found a new weapon to fight with – words. I realised the power contained in words and how just a few strung together in a sentence can change lives, either positively or negatively.

In 1839, novelist and playwright Edward Bulwer-Lytton wrote the words, *'The pen is mightier than the sword.'* I had seen proof of this in the Rap songs that I had written and recorded. I had witnessed the transforming power of songs and music in the young people that I had worked with and supported – music had transformed their lives. Now, as I started dialysis, I needed to fight a new fight. It would take a powerful weapon to keep me from falling into the pit of despair.

It had been four years since I had stopped performing as a Rapper and this had created another void, an emptiness that needed to be filled. I had been asked to play the percussion at church meetings a few times, but it wasn't enough. The combination of musical emptiness and kidney failure was already impacting my mental health, I sensed a deep loss. I would even describe it as grieving just the same as a bereavement.

All that could be done regarding my kidney failure was already being done, I could do no more. That's when I fought back with what I could, with what I knew. This time it wasn't words, it was music. I decided that it is never too late for anything. That is when I realised that if I'm still breathing, then someone somewhere will still value me. I just have to find out who and where they are.

Something inside of me urged me to search the internet and I typed – 'Find a band.' I found a website called, 'Join my band' and immediately posted a request, maybe it was more like a plea. I said something like, "Frustrated drummer seeks like-minded musicians to play Irish music or similar in the Stroud area." Apart from being half-Irish, I'm not sure why I limited my chances like that. I had never played Irish music but felt that I could give it a go. I thought perhaps I could play in a ceilidh band or find a session gathering that I might join. I believe if we take a small step of faith, God will give us even more than we anticipated and He will always provide what we need.

I needed acceptance, reassurance and friendship. I just wanted to play music, but what we want and what we need can at times be different. In this case, my need and want were met by an almost immediate response to my plea. Messages pinged back and forth between myself and Andy. He explained that he was the bass player in a reasonably new band called, 'The Shaggy Dog Raconteurs.' I didn't even know what a raconteur is so I looked it up and discovered that it's a storyteller. I thought to myself, 'I'm a storyteller.' Andy explained that the band tells shaggy dog stories in their lyrics.

I asked what sort of music it was. "Well, it's not Irish, it's Americana. I think you'll like it. I'll send you some songs we've recorded." Andy seemed very keen to get me on board and that is when the beast of imposter syndrome attacked again.

"Who am I trying to kid? They'll see right through me? I'm not a proper drummer, I just hit a box *(Cajon)* with my hands. What have I done?" My mind flooded with doubt. "Have I made a mistake?"

As I thought about the process that had brought me to this point, I realised that God had directed me and given me the courage to post my plea, only now it didn't feel like courage, it was more like stupidity. "They won't like me. I won't like them. They'll see through me. They'll think I'm a fraud. A drummer isn't a proper musician."

That last thought resonated in my head and only amplified the imposter syndrome. As I listened to the songs that Andy had sent, I found that I liked them, but that only increased the negativity toward myself. It felt as if I was on a rollercoaster that was heading for a brick wall; that would end with a crash.

"I couldn't play in a band? I had a rubber tube stuck in my gut and they're bound to notice. Why am I doing this?" I was trying to talk myself out of it, but every time I chatted with Andy, he seemed hopeful. By now we were chatting by phone and it made such a difference, we connected on a new level and he invited me to audition on Saturday 29th October, 2016. Before I thought too much and tried to convince myself to say no, I just blurted out, "OK."

Armed with directions and the three or four songs that I had listened to and played along with, I turned up at Matt's house *(or Kennel as it was referred to)*. I prayed all the way there and by the time I arrived, newfound confidence filled me. As I set up, I chatted with Bill (Billdog) , Matt (Matlee) and Andy (Bass-it Hound) and I felt amongst friends.

We played the few songs that I knew, then moved on with some new material (for me) and they liked what I could do. So much so that they asked me there and then if I would like to play with them in a few days' time at an open mic in a pub. Talk about being thrown into the deep end, I expected to go home and then receive a call saying that I failed. Again, I responded without a thought, "Yes, I'd love to."

Then, as I was packing my kit away, I thought that I needed to be completely open and honest with them. "I think I need to tell you that I've just recently started dialysis. I have a tube in my gut that comes out through my belly. I need to go home every night and attach myself to a machine."

When I finished saying my piece, they all said words like, 'That doesn't matter, you can still play can't you.' I would later realise that they each had their own struggles, as we all do and that music and the band was the therapy that they all needed. It continued to be that way for the next six years. We had all gone through tough times and have been there to support each other. During my time with the band, I received my kidney transplant, was involved in a serious accident that put me on life support and had a shoulder replacement, but they never gave up on me.

At that first open mic, we sounded great and it was such a buzz. When chatting afterwards, I commented about their dog names and asked if I could have one. I could tell from their reaction that they thought, 'Wow, he's really into this.'

"Yes, what did you have in mind?" One of them asked, I think it was Andy.

"Yellow Dog", I said and went on to explain that my surname means 'Son of Yellow Dog.' I continued with the story that 'Yellow Dog' was an Irish Celtic chieftain and that I am a direct descendant of him. They were clearly impressed and welcomed me to 'the pack.'

I feel that it's important to point out that none of these three would call themselves 'Christians.' However, I do believe God led me to them to meet my need and want. They accepted me and made me feel valued as they gave me a chance and with their support, I have become a more rounded character. I have developed more confidence; playing on stage in pubs, clubs and festivals will do that. Over the years with 'The Dogs' the lineup changed, Andy left, and Duncan and Jason joined. I am so thankful for their help, support and understanding.

This chapter is called Dog Fight or Flight for good reason and I have already mentioned that I am a fighter. Over the next two and a half years on dialysis, my fight would be taken to a new level. My resilience would be tested and pushed to the limit and I would receive a new title – 'Warrior.'

I discovered this title one day when I stumbled across the Kidney Care UK Facebook group page. All the other sufferers of kidney disease referred to each other in this way and by talking with some of them, I too joined the tribe of warriors. I battled alongside them, feeling their pain, suffering and loss. I had found another source of support. However, since I received my transplant, I have not been in the group much. I needed a break.

The problem with any support group for life-limiting health issues is although there is support, there has to be a balance. You also have to give out in return and I came to a place where I had nothing left to give, dialysis does that. You are also faced with the constant reminder that this disease kills, and you eventually die from it. In the group, I heard of people dying on more or less a weekly basis, so I stepped out for self-preservation.

I have no doubt that at some point in the future, I will need to return, but for now, I have friends that support and that includes The Shaggy Dog Raconteurs.

At the start of 2020, as a band, we were out on the road at least every other weekend and the momentum was growing. Then the Covid pandemic hit and venues were closed across the country. We stayed creative by recording in our own homes and creating music by file sharing via the internet, but we would never hit the peak of where we were pre-pandemic. Outdoor gigs became the new way, but after two years, my body felt weary. In May 2022, I was struggling with angina again and required 3 more cardio stents. I started to feel like I was letting the band down.

Just two months later, in July, we played at Chalfest, a 5,000-capacity festival and it took it out of me. Sadly, that was the last time that I played with The Shaggy Dog Raconteurs, at a debrief afterwards I stepped down. It was a tough decision and I do miss playing with my friends. True friendship never dies and I am still in contact with all of the band and still help and support them in other creative ways. When I announced my departure from the band, I felt God was leading me and once again telling me that 'I'm still valued.'

Playing with The Shaggy Dog Raconteurs

Consider this…

1. Are you a worrier or a warrior?

   Do you fight or flight?

2. I am tenacious – What one positive word
   can you hold onto for yourself?

3. What have you lost?

What part of your life are you grieving for?

4. Have you found a support group that values you yet?

5. Have you started a new activity yet?

6. What new purpose and identity can you seek for your own life?

Chapter Nine
The waiting game

Any expectant parents who have had to wait longer than the usual nine months of pregnancy will tell you that every day over the predicted delivery date is an anxious day. After two weeks of being overdue, the anxiety has intensified and the risk to the unborn child increases. Thankfully, medical intervention is available to bring the struggle to an end. A date is set, procedures are carried out and the waiting game ends. It's a common scenario that we can relate to as many of us have experienced it or know someone that has.

Imagine a prisoner who is waiting on death row in the USA. They have been there for years. They may be completely innocent, having been wrongly convicted and so they have a right to an appeal, called the *'Direct Appeal.'*

Some prisoners will be granted an opportunity for two more appeals, the State Post-Conviction and Federal Habeas Corpus. Finally, there is a last chance for reprieve if the State Governor chooses to grant Executive Clemency.

This process takes years and it is a waiting game, with an unknown end date and a meeting with death. Each new appeal brings with it fresh hope. Each prisoner clings to that hope, as hope extinguishes fear, fear of the inevitable – death.

The expectant parents and the death row prisoner are two different scenarios. Both have been thrown into a waiting game. Which one do you think most resembles the waiting game? The agony of prolonged anxiety, biding your time whilst your life is on hold? During this constant state of anticipation, in reality, you're actually 'hoping' that someone else, *(with a compatible kidney)*, dies.

Just stop and process that for a minute or two.

If surviving until a suitable transplant becomes available is a long and painful process, holding on to the chance of finding the alternative, *(a living donor)*, is a much longer affair and is extremely unlikely to be a positive one.

The parents know what they are going to get and when they are going to get it, but it still seems to take forever. The prisoner knows the likely outcome but in contrast, they long for it to be delayed. Waiting for a transplant is something akin to that of the experience of that prisoner. Every night I was a prisoner in my own bedroom, attached to a machine. Days come and go and you wait with an expectant state of readiness, in preparation for when the phone would ring.

At this juncture, travel is restricted to within a limited distance from your transplant centre. In my case that was Oxford. You never know when the waiting game will end. It could be two days or an unknown number of years. It could end well or you might die. Try to imagine what that might feel like. I know that you would find this very difficult because I couldn't envisage anything until I had to play the game for real, this horrible game – the waiting game.

In a similar way that the prisoner has a chance of an appeal and is lifted by hope, the phone rings. A nurse tells me that they may have a kidney. A surge of hope rushes through me and tears fill my eyes as a flood of emotion overwhelms my brain. For me, during my three-year sentence in the waiting game, the phone rang five times. That is the equivalent of five appeal hearings.

I was added to the transplant waiting list in February 2016, along with the other 5,000 people. That is when my unknown wait started, my jail sentence, my waiting game. I waited 17 months before that first call, every day praying, every day hopeful. Then, on 17th July 2017, I thought that it was finally all over. The nurse first told me who she was and where she was calling from. She asked me to confirm my name and date of birth, all the usual routine identity checks. My heart instantly tried to leap from my chest as she told me that they may have a possible kidney match. Then it sank, dropped like a stone as she explained, "You are second on the list, that means you are on standby. There's no need to do anything, but please don't eat or drink. We will call you later if you need to come to the hospital."

As soon as she hung up, confusion hit me. No one had even mentioned that the protocol was to always have another potential recipient. On that day I learned that for every deceased donor, four people on the waiting list are called, two for each kidney. A new waiting game started for me, one that I thought would be over soon, one that was even more intense. It lasted over 14 hours and I was starving. Friends had been contacted and people were praying, but the phone didn't ring. I couldn't wait any longer, so decided to call them back and was given an apology. They forgot to call me. They left me hanging on all day and forgot to stand me down. I learnt some hard lessons that day, though the whole experience did give me a short-lived hope.

I tried to convince myself that the waiting could be over soon because they had at least started to call me, but it didn't work like that. I suppose it's a little bit like waiting for your lottery numbers to come up, the odds are massively stacked against you. It would be another 13 months and four more calls before this current season of misery would end. For all I knew at that moment in time, it could have been much longer.

You may be thinking that I am over-exaggerating my emotional feelings with that call, so let me explain a little more about where my mind was before they phoned. As I approached the first-year anniversary of being on the waiting list and playing the game, I had also been on dialysis for six months. My mind was in a very dark place. I was having thoughts such as, 'Life isn't worth living.'

Every night as I prepared to attach to my machine, the darkness closed in on me. Even now, writing this memory triggers the feelings, they were so powerful and overwhelming. Tears would often roll down my face as I scrubbed up, but I managed to hide them from Heather. At one stage I remember being overcome with a sense of grief at the thought that someone would have to die so that I could live.

It's very easy and also possibly cynical to read this now and say, "That is what Jesus did for you." I know that, of course, I do. I knew it then, but in that darkness that engulfs and consumes you, it's easy to lose sight of that glimmer of light. That is why some people take their own lives. They are so consumed with torment, that they see only one way out. I know this. I mentioned in my book *'The Golden Thread,'* that I was first suicidal at the age of 14.

As I alluded to earlier, the darkest time for me during this season came one night as the thought around the raw facts of the transplant process were rammed home. Someone has to die! The thought changed into, 'What if one of my children had to die? What if they were to be *my* deceased donor?'

This thought was becoming very active as it started to infect my mind every night. It was a devastating reflection that I just couldn't shake off. I dreaded going to bed because I knew that the monster of debilitating anxiety would attack. It would take me about half an hour to get ready for bed, attach to my machine and go through the physical drain pain. I was usually in bed by the time Heather came up and managed to wipe away my tears, compose myself temporarily and disguise my true feelings.

As soon as the lights went out, the monster crawled around in my stomach. Physical pain caused by anxiety is a real thing and I pulled my knees up and curled up into a ball. In the darkness, I cried myself to sleep. I did it silently so as not to raise Heather's attention. Hiding my true feelings *(or at least I thought I was),* only made the problem worse and I would grab my head with my hands.

My nails often dug deep into my scalp. It was a physical pain to mask the emotional pain. I knew enough to know that this was a mild form of self-harm and could ultimately end in suicide.

Some mornings when I woke, I noticed the dried blood under my fingernails and I scrubbed up in haste, before disconnecting from my machine. I was free again.

My life had been saved that day because I phoned the Samaritans and talked. What's great was the simple fact that the person on the end of the phone listened. I learned something that day, talking about a problem can save your life.

I knew that I had to be honest with Heather, so eventually I told her how it was. I maybe didn't share all the details, but enough for her to realise that I needed help. I confided with one of my nurses and she said, "I'm not surprised to hear this, but please understand that you have done well. Most people hit this wall much earlier. You have managed over a year without any support for your mental health. We have a clinical psychologist as part of our team. Would you like to see her?"

A fresh hope surged through me. She understood. I had shared my feelings and no longer felt alone. Help was available and offered to me. In the space of three months from March to May 2018, I attended four sessions and things did slightly improve, although it may have also been the anti-depressants that I had been prescribed.

When you play this waiting game, resilience gets thinner and it doesn't take much to drop you back into the pit of despair. That first phone call lifted my hopes high, only to be dropped back into the pile of 5,000 other people that are also playing the same game. It was no surprise to find myself back in the battle with that beast that is anxiety. I had won the previous battle but was losing the war and two months after that first call, I sat in the chair opposite the clinical psychologist in an even worse state.

I remember around the same time speaking to my renal consultant and I said I don't know how much more of this I can take. His bedside manner was not the best and he offered me the option of coming off of dialysis and letting the disease kill me. He explained that they could make my end comfortable. It shocked me and I reacted by saying, "I don't want to die." As I look back now, I believe his abrupt manner brought me to a turning point. Instead of helping me to end my life, I was referred back to the psychologist for three more sessions.

During this time, I also began to channel some of my anguish into poetry and I'll share a couple here. I hope you like them and I hope they help you to understand my state of mind.

Anxiety

Anxiety came again last night!
I thought he had gone forever.
I was wrong,
thought I was free,
and thought that I was better.

Anxiety just waits,
waiting to strike.
Patient until the dark of night.
I first hear his breathing, snorting,
powerful and loud.
Followed quickly by the rush
of the crowd.
Rushing, crushing,
consuming, controlling.
Too late,
I have gone,
Anxiety has won.
He has won,

though the battle has just begun.

I fight.
Naturally, I fight.
Fight or flight?
I always chose fight.
Wrestling with all of my might.

The blows come hard.
He attacks my head.
He wants me dead.

My desperate whimpers,
a pitiful sound.
Need to find the solid ground.
Tossing and turning.
Hot then cold.
Soaking, sweating.
Time to be bold.
Two hours of struggle
have left me weak.
Have I reached my defeat?
I find something to help me sleep.
I awake again to another day.
Anxiety has gone,
thank God I pray.

What I want for Christmas

What I want for Christmas,
what I really would adore.
I want the same as last year and the year before.
It's not just what I want, It's what I really need.
But for anyone to have this,
someone needs to bleed.
I'm not alone in waiting,
5,000 want the same.
Just waiting and a waiting,
it's called "the waiting game".
It really is the greatest gift,
that anyone could give.
Your sacrifice is more than nice,
you give a chance to live.
So what is this gift so precious?
What then can it be?
If you can please spare one,
I need a new kidney.
If you would like to leave this gift,
after you have gone.
Just register now,
tell your family,
but please don't wait too long.
For some, if they don't have this gift,
the pain will make them cry.

And all that they can do,
is watch the time go by.
They wait and then they die.
What I want for Christmas,
is a kidney transplant, that's what.
I think if I don't have one soon,
I might just lose the plot.

Consider this...

1. We all have giants; it doesn't matter if yours are bigger or smaller than mine.

   The thing to learn from this chapter is that I didn't face my giants alone. If I had, I would not have survived.

2. Who do you talk to and share your burdens?

3. Do you find it useful to share your struggles?

4. It doesn't have to be poetry, but write down how you are struggling and feeling.

   Share it with someone that you trust.

Chapter Ten
Don't Give Up Hope

As I start to write this chapter, I have just tested positive for Covid-19. I am trying to write in between some very bad shivers but it isn't easy. With my immune system suppressed, it could develop into something quite serious. I am currently waiting for medication to help fight it off and people are praying for me all around the world.

The warrior in me says, 'Don't give up, fight this', so I write. Even with this new health complication, I am still valued and I can continue to share my story. Before I continue, please know that whatever your situation, whatever ailments you are battling, God can and will still use you. You are still valued.

*****

Six months after my first transplant call and almost two years of the waiting game, another glimmer of hope came my way. In January 2018, a friend offered to be tested as a potential living donor. This is a huge ask of anyone and I did try to talk them out of it. Nevertheless, they insisted and we visited the transplant centre together. I really didn't know how to respond to such a generous offer. When the conclusion of the tests came back as unsuitable, I didn't know whether to sigh with relief *(for them AND for my potential guilt towards them)* or, cry for the hope that had once again been ripped away from me. The waiting game truly is an emotional roller coaster and you wonder every day if you will jump off; before crashing into the wall at the end.

Another well-meaning friend approached me just four months later to be considered as a living donor. We went through the same procedure of tests and interviews, only to be told yet again that they were not suitable. I simply cannot describe the emotions that I felt after these two events. The thought of these two people being prepared to undergo life-threatening major surgery and give a physical part of themselves, takes a lot of courage, compassion and love.

God loves the world so much that He gave us His one and only Son and as Christians, we are all called to be like Jesus. These two potential living donors were both Christian friends and they were demonstrating their selflessness and willingness to help me in my moment of need. I look back to this time and question, what price are we prepared to pay to help a fellow human being?

After yet another letdown, I needed to find another weapon for this battle – all warriors need weapons. In the same way that I had sought out The Shaggy Dog Raconteurs, I now discovered Longfield Care. I had known where they were based for decades, as they ran a hospice just up the road from me. However, like many other misinformed people, I thought that a hospice was where you go to die.

As I searched their website, I was re-educated and found out that the majority of their patients don't die *(well not for a long time anyway)*. Their slogan is 'Live well and die well with a life-limiting illness.' My illness was limiting me and I wanted to live well. When I first entered the building, I felt like a fraud. I didn't have cancer and I could clearly see that others were in a worse state than me. One man carried an oxygen bottle wherever he went, whilst others were visibly struggling. My illness and therefore my disabilities were invisible, but the staff treated us all with the same dignity and respect.

I accessed a six-week course on dealing with

breathlessness and fatigue. Serious fatigue is painful, it is far more than just extreme tiredness. Every single muscle throughout my entire body hurt. There were some parts of the course that I didn't like, mindfulness with its Buddhist roots did not appeal to me. I referred to it as 'mindlessness' because the process involves emptying your mind. I wouldn't do it, as I always want God in my head.

The main thing that did help me was peer support and seeing others in much worse conditions. I had always said that no matter how bad a situation becomes, there will always be someone in a far worse place.

I was supported by Longfield for over a year, right beyond my transplant. Massage therapy helped to improve my dialysis and art therapy helped to prevent my head from filling with dark thoughts. I also accessed the NHS mental health service called 'Let's Talk.'

A year after that first potential transplant phone call, something else happened. I would refer to it as a revelation or even a miracle, but I'll save that story for the next chapter.

My second transplant call came after two years of being on the waiting list. It was the same as the first call, stay home and wait. This time it seemed easier, I had more resilience and more support. They also stood me down quickly and I just continued with life as it was.

I waited another eleven months before the phone rang again. This time I was called to the Oxford transplant centre, but only as the secondary patient. I waited all day, only to be sent home again.

Just ten days later, the same happened again, only this time I was the primary candidate - first in the queue. We were supposed to be going away for the weekend with the church but we had to cancel the trip and asked them all to pray.

My hope had been built up. I was prepped for surgery, gowned up, with a canular in my vein. I even had a separate room with a hospital bed and I was nil by mouth. My expectations were high, adrenalin filled my body ready for the fight of surgery. Fear had been dispelled by the hope that surged through every fibre of my very being. Can you imagine the tension that I faced?

This turned into the longest wait of my four false calls and you guessed it, I was sent home again, but the reason why caused an emotional overload. The surgeon himself came in to break the news. He explained that, even though the deceased person was an organ donor, the family still had the final say. They had taken too long to give their consent and the kidneys were wasted, no good to anyone.

I learned that day that this can happen all too often. Families hesitate in the emotional shock and no good comes from the death of their loved one. When the surgeon broke the news, I wept.

At last, my fifth and final call came soon after. The waiting game was over, but this is also another chapter.

Consider this…

1. In the UK, the law has now been updated. Everyone is now considered to be an organ donor unless the person has opted out. However, relatives STILL have the final say. If you want your organs to be

used to help another after you have gone,
be sure to let your relatives know now.

Chapter Eleven
I'm Still Valued

So, what about that revelation I referred to just now? Was it in fact, a miracle? This event took place in July 2018, after I had been on the transplant waiting list for two years and five months. I was still on dialysis. Cast your mind back to chapter three, the story of the person who told me I could never be an author. I had struggled to break through that barrier, to overcome the curse and call myself an author. This is the story of how that curse was broken.

We went to a Christian summer camp festival, called, "Naturally Supernatural." This was our third year of attending. Halfway through the week, during the loud worship time, in the throng of thousands of people, I became angry with God. I sat and I cried out aloud, "O God! What am I supposed to be doing with my life? Have you given up on me? Do you no longer have any use for me? Why have you abandoned me?" That is what it felt like.

Then, in the midst of the noise and hubbub, I heard Him! It wasn't an audible voice; it was like a brain download. Some may say that it was a thought, but it was so much more than that. It originated from a supernatural source! It was so powerful I was shaking, **"You still have skills and tools that I have given you. I want you to use them. I haven't finished with you yet."**

I felt the warming presence of the Holy Spirit coursing through me and I instantly knew that God had heard my cry and had responded. However, I still didn't know what it meant. Skills and tools? Did He want me to continue in youth work? He had equipped me for that role, but now it didn't seem right.

Later that week, a woman whom I had never met before was praying for me. She told me that she felt that God hadn't finished with me yet. She had a picture of me walking and said, "I believe God wants you to walk with your Gospel shoes on and that you will be ready to speak the good news of the Gospel."

For a brief period, once again I found myself angry and confused. I tried to explain to her, "I have end-stage kidney failure, I'm on dialysis and I'm waiting for a transplant! I don't think

I'll be walking far anytime soon!" My reaction to her was a perfect indicator of how frustrated I was feeling with my whole life at that point. My tone was hurtful and attacking.

I was bang out of order, yet she humbly apologised, "I'm sorry, I'm new to this and maybe I have it wrong?"

We both returned to our seats, but something caused me to watch where she went. She was four rows immediately behind where I was sitting. Her words continued to echo around my head, just like the words from five years earlier had stayed with me, *"You can never be an author!"*

She said, *"God hasn't finished with you yet!"* God had told me the same, *"I haven't finished with you yet!"* Little did I know, this was the five-year-old curse being undone, I was being released. ***"I have given you tools and skills..."***

My mind raced through my life, *'What tools? What skills?'* My thoughts galloped backwards and stopped in the first year of knowing Jesus. Instantly I knew what He was telling me. I rushed over to the woman who had prayed for me. "I'm so sorry", I said, "I need to apologise.

God spoke to me through you and I was too angry to hear or understand, but what you said was spot on. I now know that he wants me to write."

In my first year of knowing Jesus, He gave me the gift *(tool)* and the ability *(skill),* of rhyming words and I used it to become a Christian Rap artist. That skill has since developed and my writing skills *(storytelling),* helped me to develop The Door Youth Project charity.

I could feel the power of the Holy Spirit already forming words in my head and I was so excited. When I went home from Naturally Supernatural, I had the idea to write some teen fiction. I had previously gathered a collection of teen fiction books, which I now intended to read, in order to gain inspiration. Now, as I pawed my way through the books, I came to an abrupt halt, as I once again heard God's voice in my heart, *"I have given you the tools and skills, now use them!"*

So, I left the books on the shelf, then, doubt tried to have the final word. *"You can NEVER be an author! An author writes 3,600 words an hour!"* Was that actually true? I decided to Google it and discovered that most authors write 1,000 words in a day. That was when I found a reference to the figure of 3,600. This, apparently, is how many words a copy typist can produce in an hour. An element of truth had been injected into a convincing lie. I had been cursed and lied to. I now knew the truth and I started to write my first novel. "Issues" was written in just over a month and published in January 2019. Then, as soon as it was published, I felt inspired to write, 'My Foundation for Life' *(published February 2019)*. I had used the skills and the tools, but still struggled to call myself an author *(the curse was strong)* – *"You can never be an author!"* The fire was fading in my heart and I didn't write much apart from poetry *(recovering from a kidney transplant slowed me down)*. Then at the end of my transplant year in November 2019, I realised that I had written enough poems for my first poetry book, so I published 'Rhyme Time'. I questioned if poetry qualified me as an author. The all-encompassing Imposter syndrome consumed me again and I convinced myself, *'I can never be an author'*.

At the beginning of 2020, the weather turned. As it started to snow, I was once again inspired to write my first science fiction novel. I was halfway through writing it, when I had a serious accident *(story coming later)*, and so I stopped writing again. When 'The INVASION of the MIMICS', my fifth book, was eventually published in October 2020, I could, at last, call myself an *'author'*. The curse had been lifted and with it came a full-on release.

I must also mention another significant step that helped to remove the curse. In January 2020, I discovered and joined the Association of Christian Writers. In doing so I realised that I was not alone. I had struggled to believe in myself due to working in isolation, but that was no longer the case. I found so many supportive and understanding new friends in the ACW, many of whom had also struggled with imposter syndrome. Peer support is essential for all of us and my new-found peers were now referring to me as an author.

Just after publishing 'The Invasion of the Mimics, I was in a prayer meeting, when these words came into my head, "ONE GOD – Many names." I instantly thought that I had to produce a film *(yes, I also make films),* with this title. As the film was being made, I knew that

God also wanted me to publish a book with the same title. So in November 2020, I started to meditate on the many names and titles of God. There are over 900 in the book. As I wrote my thoughts and life-related stories, I could feel God's Holy Spirit's presence growing in me. Then, after just three months and halfway through writing the book, he gave me another 'commission'.

Commission is the word that I like to use. I see it as **COM**e together on **MISSION** with God. This time, the call was to use the 'base' writing skill that he had given me *(use the skills and tools)* – 'rhyme'. A friend of mine had recently written Psalm 23 as a rhyming poem. I had produced a poetry book and several *'spoken word'* films. Now, I felt God speak to me again, **"I gave you these tools and these skills for this time, everything else that you have written was in preparation for this project. Work with me and write the "Psalms in Rhyme."**

I write to bless others and to give God the glory and so I was obedient and did as he had commanded. So, in February 2021, I also started working on 'Psalms in Rhyme.' When I started, the speed at which I was writing told me that the whole book, with 2,461 verses, would take two and a half years. I remember actually saying to God, "Really? You're having a laugh, aren't you?" In response, I felt God speak into my heart again, **"Just let me show you."**

Once again, I felt the Holy Spirit touch me, reassure me and reveal the words to write. Instead of two and a half years, it took just over six months before it was written and published. That was a miracle and at times, I couldn't write the words down fast enough. The writing was now flowing, like a supernatural river of words. The curse was broken, "I AM AN AUTHOR!"

Writing two books at the same time is quite incredible and only possible for me with God in the mix. Also, as if that wasn't enough, he gave me my first illustrated children's book to produce, *'The Land of Make Believe.'* He continued to pour other poems into my mind regularly, plus he gave me the first four chapters of the sequel to, *'The Invasion of the Mimics'* called *'Legacy of the Mimics.'* All this in the space of a few months.

Just a few negative words telling me that *'I CAN'T'* had held me back, but I had learned.

NEVER believe it when ANYONE tells you that you can't do something or be something. ALWAYS reject the NEGATIVE words spoken over you.

Consider this...

1. What tools and skills do you still have that God can use?

2. What or who is stopping you from using them?

Chapter Twelve
Transplant

I leapt forward quite a bit in that last chapter to cover the journey of becoming an author, but let's return to my renal failure journey. On 23rd February 2019, after a three-year wait. The phone eventually rang for the last time.

This was the call that I had been waiting for.

On that day we had planned a rare gathering of Heather's side of her family. A buffet lunch had been prepared and just as the first people arrived to eat, the phone rang. The nurse on the end of the line told me that I was 'nil by mouth' and to make my way to Oxford as soon as possible.

Within a few minutes, my bag was packed and we left the food and guests to eat and lock up when they left. We had travelled the road many times previously and knew that it would take an hour and twenty minutes on a clear run.

I now realise that life rarely gives us clear runs. Is that being negative or realistic? We hit the tailback and almost stopped, crawling along before we faced the policeman parked across the road. The main A40 approach to Oxford was blocked due to an accident. We needed to seek an alternative route along with everyone else.

I'm pretty sure everyone in the traffic jam was frustrated, but how many of them had been waiting three years for a life-saving moment in time? The diversion involved driving over an ancient toll bridge, where the queue crawled along. A man sat in a booth at the mid-point of the bridge collecting five pence from each car. Did we even have any money? We must have had because we were allowed to pass and eventually, we arrived at the hospital about an hour later than anticipated.

I questioned God, "Why does life need to be so complicated?" Little did I know then that there would be even more complications ahead. It is possible to receive a kidney transplant and be home five days later. This stay in the hospital would be eleven days before they discharged me.

Various tests took place throughout the remainder of the afternoon. At some point, a doctor told me that it was going to be a very long wait, so I should grab a snack. I was starving and when they bought me a sandwich, I did as I was told and gratefully consumed it. An hour later, I was informed that they were now ready for me. I explained I had just eaten, and was therefore told that I would have to wait another six hours. I simply couldn't believe what I was hearing and moaned about the doctor who recommended that I have some food. This was so very frustrating, but you can imagine that it would be even more so at this juncture. Remember, there is only a small window of opportunity before the organ becomes unusable. I was understandably distressed.

Anyway, I went to surgery at 11.00 pm and received the new kidney with just thirty minutes to spare! The operation was a success, but due to the delay, the kidney was referred to as sleepy. This *'delayed graft'* needed to be woken up. To put it simply, it wasn't working. My body was filling with fluid and the only way it was going to go was with dialysis, so I was manually drained three times each day for three days.

To make matters even worse, my bowel had been disturbed during surgery and I developed my second life-threatening paralytic ileus. The young student nurse with me at the time, reacted with complete shock as black vomit projected across the room and splattered the wall opposite. It was violent and probably the first time that she had observed such an event.

I managed to instruct her speaking quickly, "I have a paralytic ileus. I need an NG tube stat. Call a doctor now." My previous experience had taught me the lingo and the urgency and a doctor appeared immediately, with a tube inserted within ten minutes.

I try to find the humour in the darkest of moments and when the nurse first reacted, she found me a standard sick bowl. I glanced quickly at the bowl, then toward her and screamed, "You're gonna need a bigger bowl." It reminded me of that scene in the movie 'Jaws' where someone says, "We're gonna need a bigger boat!"

I now had five different tubes inserted into my body *(2 drains, my dialysis catheter, my willie catheter and an NG tube)* and I looked a right state. The room and bed looked like I had exploded, but as I sat there in my own mess, I knew that God still valued me and that He hadn't finished with me yet.

Over the eleven days in the hospital, a stream of compassionate friends came to visit and it was so good to see them. Although visitors can be tiring, I feel that they also help toward the healing process.

When I eventually returned home, I chatted with my neighbour and he told me that his dad had recently died. His cause of death was a 'paralytic ileus'. It certainly highlighted the severity of what I had been through.

As people found out about my transplant, they were genuinely happy for me and many of them said, "You are cured then?"

I lost count of the number of times that I had to explain, it's not a cure, there is no cure, it's just another treatment. The transplant works, but due to the delay it has never risen much above 30% function, it has been working for over four years and I am currently no longer in need of dialysis.

Some Christians reading this may be wondering if I have ever forgiven the doctor who told me to eat. I would say that I have, as I hold no bitterness or resentment toward him. The fact that I did eventually receive my transplant filled me with so much joy and hope that I was grateful for the entire team that had cared for me. It does none of us any good to hold grudges. I am just happy to be alive.

I had survived my second close brush with death, I had to consume a pile of pills for the rest of my life, my immune system had been suppressed, my white blood cells were low and I was labelled, 'Clinically Extremely Vulnerable' – CEV. On top of all of that, Covid was coming.

I still live with chronic kidney disease *(CKD)*, and I still have huge native polycystic kidneys *(PKD)*. This illness is still life-limiting and disabling, yet I am still able, I am capable and I am still valued.

Consider this...

1. On a scale of 1-10 how valued do you feel?

2. List out the negative things and thoughts that make you feel devalued.

3. List out the positive things that could make you feel valued.

4. We all have things that we perceive as negative in our lives but we need a good balance.

   What positive angle or twist can you put on the negative perceptions?

   How can you pray to reduce or eliminate the negative?

5. Find a helpful friend to support you in this. Remember, my hospital visitors were like a lifeline to me.

Chapter Thirteen
Crash, bang, wallop

After the long three-year wait and two and a half years on dialysis, the transplant provided an element of freedom. Life seemed to almost return to normal and for sixteen months I had no serious hospital visits. There were of course the regular check-ups and post-transplant procedures, but nothing too traumatic. Looking back, it seemed to be a much-needed reprieve and we made the most of life.

As mentioned earlier in the chapter about The Shaggy Dog Raconteurs, we were becoming more well-known as a band, travelling further afield and playing at gigs every other weekend. On 14th March 2020, we played at a venue in Wales, but there was a very strange atmosphere. Covid was being mentioned, fear was spreading and just over a week later, lockdown was enforced upon the UK.

I received notification immediately telling me that, as I am a transplant recipient and classed as Clinically Extremely Vulnerable *(CEV)*, I had to 'shield.' To be told to confine yourself to your own home for 3 months was bad news, but of course, it had to be done. Once again, I was a prisoner and Heather was trapped with me.

We all quickly learned how to use online meeting platforms and church adapted as we all met online.

My brother had the same kidney disease as me, with additional heart complications and sadly he died just before the lockdown. With restricted numbers of mourners allowed at funerals and my shielding situation, I was advised not to attend the funeral. This was the first real indicator of just how difficult this whole process was going to be.

Part of my mental health coping mechanism is to write. So, I produced a series of spoken word videos called 'My Lockdown Series.' My body fitness also allowed me to do some much-needed work on the house. I could still order materials for delivery.

We had been used to adjusting to health situations rapidly and we adapted quickly to the new, lockdown conditions as well. Where the general population struggled with things such as hand washing and mask-wearing, I was already used to these guidelines because of my condition. Lockdown became just another norm.

By June 2020, I was allowed to leave the house to collect goods that I had ordered online *(click & collect)*. So, on 8th June 2020, I left the house to fetch a tube of decorator filler. Little did I know that that purchase could have cost me my life.

I live on a very steep and narrow country lane. I step from the gate straight into the road, there are no pavements. My view is obscured by my neighbour's overgrown hedge. One step, two steps, smash! The speeding cyclist made no sound and seemed to come out of nowhere. The human missile hit me with force. I felt my feet leave the ground and in a whirling blur, I landed some five metres away further down the hill. I later found out that the cyclist first hit our car, which was parked on the road. That helped to reduce the impact on me. It all happened so fast, too fast to notice the small details.

The initial impact hit me on my right side. During my short flight, my body twisted and I landed on my right side providing a secondary impact and more wounds. From my waist to my head, I sustained multiple injuries. Firstly, my transplant kidney is situated just above my pelvis on my right. It had suffered major trauma. Although I wasn't aware, my kidney function was already dropping. It would soon be at 10% *(end-stage)* and I would be prepped for dialysis. I struggled to breathe with six broken ribs, I felt my whole rib cage moving. The pain was unbearable. I had sustained a fractured right wrist but other pains were so severe it wasn't noticed straight away. My right shoulder was a mess, dislocated, and broken in two places and my bicep tendon had ruptured beyond repair. Blood trickled from a wound on my head. The bones to the side of my right eye socket crunched when I touched them. I also drifted in and out of consciousness with a concussion.

I remember being led on my back, head facing downhill for what seemed an eternity. I remember my clothes being cut from my body by paramedics. The gas and air helped with the pain but my head spun even more. I remember the fire and rescue service being there due to the narrow access. I remember the neck brace being fitted to keep my head in position. Most of all I remember the surge of pain as my broken body was gently manoeuvred onto a spine board.

I assume I was placed into the waiting ambulance but I just can't remember. I don't remember the journey to the hospital and I have no recollection of being in the emergency department, but I know that I was there. I took a photograph of me there and posted it on social media, but can't remember doing so. I also don't remember having any X-rays, yet I know several were taken. I later found out about the damage to my kidney but have no memory of a CT scan. I was transferred to a ward but failed to even remember that.

Due to Covid, no one was allowed to travel with me to the hospital and no visitors were allowed. All Heather could do was wait for the information that she received by phone. I was told that I was on the ward for two days before being taken to the operating theatre, although there is one thing that I can recall about that time.

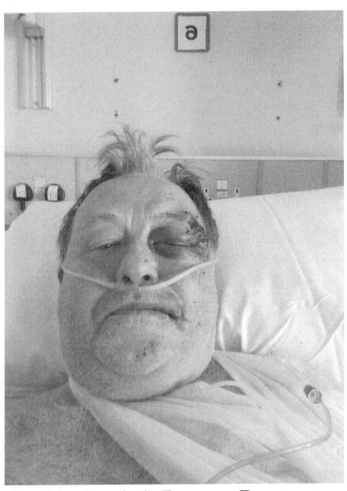

Proof that I was in the Emergency Department
and bloated from years of steroids

One of my friends happens to be the hospital
Chaplain. No visitors were allowed during this
time, but I do remember him coming to see me

every day that he was in the hospital. I can't remember much of what we talked about either, but I was so pleased to see a friendly and familiar face. I am sure that my mind was trying to shut down due to the extreme lack of familiarity, combined with immense pain.

In the operating theatre, they reset my dislocated shoulder. I'm not sure whether they were planning to repair the two shoulder breaks at the same time, as their plans had to change. Whilst under general anaesthetic, I experienced an aspiration. This is when something enters and obstructs your airway. My stomach contents had apparently caused the problem and I woke up two days later on a life support machine. The machine breathed for me and kept me alive.

During these days, my family and friends prayed. They had been told to expect the worst. My likelihood of survival was extremely low. Remember, no one could visit. I wouldn't have even been aware if they did. The struggle for Heather must have been so tough. I often think that I had the easy part, as I had absolutely no awareness, or did I?

I started to have a realisation that my eyes were

open but I couldn't speak. I have no idea when it began, but it seemed to go on for hours. The same images repeated, as if on a loop over and over. I could hear muffled voices speaking to me. A nurse with red hair walked from his desk, looked straight into my face, spoke to me and then went back to sit down. He sat a few seconds before the loop started all over again. The repetition was like torture. It could have been minutes or days that I experienced this phenomenon, but when they eventually woke me up, I recognised the nurse and knew that he was real.

As I awoke from my induced slumber, I could not speak until the tube down my throat was removed. I can't remember my first words, but I do remember being disorientated. Noises from machines overpowered the atmosphere. A doctor talked loudly to colleagues in a doorway and I remember shouting to him to shut up. The staff tried to calm me down but my brain was unable to comprehend the severity of my predicament. They decided to call Heather and allow her to see me. She was masked and gowned and had to follow a strict Covid protocol. She could only stay for a short time. We held hands and she spoke. Her voice gave me a reality check and a tear trickled down my cheek. I think that I apologised for making such a mess and causing her so much grief.

I felt something pulling on the right side of my neck, so reached my left hand up to feel the central line ready for emergency dialysis. I knew what it was and what it meant and asked if my kidney was okay. Did I need dialysis? It was then that they informed me about my damaged transplant, it had dropped to 10% function but was miraculously bouncing back up. A few minutes later, the central line was removed and I felt relief.

Shortly afterwards, I was transferred back to the ward. I remember being there for about another week and the Chaplain continued to be my visiting life-saver nearly every day. It wasn't until I was released from the hospital that I found out that many people had been praying for me. I thank each of them, whoever they may be and believe that I am alive today because of their prayers. Through the power of God, I had survived another close brush with death, in response to the cries of the saints.

The road to recovery was long and rocky. I was

discharged with a serious bowel infection, C-Difficile and nurses had to come in to take tests each day. For three months Heather helped me with toilet functions and showering, and I slept propped up in a spare bed.

I waited 21 months before I was eventually allowed to undergo surgery to have my shoulder repaired. Covid closed operating theatres, my surgeon caught Covid and I had to have cardio stents fitted before they would risk any strain on my heart. The delays resulted in further deterioration of my shoulder, as the unsecured broken bones rubbed against each other and ground themselves away. By the time I went to surgery, the shoulder was so damaged that I needed a joint replacement.

This whole story reminds me of a song from the early 90s by a band called Chumbawanba. The song is called, *'I get knocked down, but I get up again'* and this is exactly what I needed to do. Once again, I turned to writing poetry and *'When'* was the first thing that I wrote. Shortly afterwards I also wrote *'Thankful'* so here they are.

When

This is the first thing that I wrote,
following a near-fatal accident.
It was a close brush with death and of course, death
does come knocking at our door eventually.
It's only a matter of WHEN

Crash,
smash,
over in a flash.
Head took a bash.
Nasty gash.
Ribs all broken.
Shoulder explosion.
Memory erosion.
Much confusion.
Operation.
Complication.
Life support.
Hello Mort.
Life too short.
No more thought.
No more light.
Need to fight.
Survive the night.
Such a messed-up sight.

Need to stay alive.
Feed the spirit inside.
So close,
I cried.
Thankful to be alive.
You never know
WHEN,
it might happen to you,
but death will come knocking.
You all know it's true,
but before it does,
there's one thing you must do.
Believe,
repent,
invite HIM in.
No more live a life of SIN.
Be protected by the
armour of Him.
Be protected by His spirit within.

Thankful

God gave me the start of this poem
when I was in an MRI machine.

I feel so grateful, so thankful,
glad to be alive.
They say, 'Only the strong survive'.
I don't feel strong,
feel quite weak.
Struggle walking down the street,
but I'm thankful,
thankful to be alive.
Injured and deprived.
The pain lies deep inside.
Look at me the cripple.
You judge me with your fickle mind.
Open your eyes, stop acting blind.
I'm no superhero, don't wear a cape.
Tell me where to go, show me where's my fate?

See that I'm still capable and wholly available.
I thank you God and say amen.
Escaped the grip of death again.
Still, I face the struggle and pain.
Enough to make you go insane.
Oh why, oh why do I feel so bad?
I know, it's you, stops me going mad.

And I thank you again,
despite the pain.

Thank you for your grace,
That keeps me alive.
I look upon your face,
as you help me survive.
Above the noise of the MRI machine,
I hear your voice like a tambourine.
I question,
is this real or a dream?

Then I thank you, Lord,
for I am redeemed.
I thank you for your resurrection,
and giving me a special connection.
Watch over me,
give me protection.
Show me the way,
give me direction.
Now keep me safe from the flame.
I pray all this in Jesus name.
Amen is all that's left to say.
So be it, that is what I pray.

Consider this...

1. Write your own poem or try journalling to describe something about you or a and give thanks.

   Pray first and allow the Holy Spirit to guide you (a poem doesn't have to rhyme)

2. Share your writing with at least one person.

   If you are able, share it with a larger group.

3. Accept the positive comments and allow them to inspire you to write more.

Chapter Fourteen
Keep Breathing

My polycystic kidneys are rather large, I always explain to people that it is like being in the last month of pregnancy and expecting twins. The only difference is, that my term will not end without medical intervention and that will not happen unless my native kidneys become a threat to my life. So, my body continues to grow and people often make the assumption that I am fat. I am classed as overweight, and obese even, but a vast amount of my excess size is due to my kidneys.

It is easy to lose your body confidence and I often feel the need to explain to people why I am so big. On one occasion I was waiting to go on stage at a festival with the band. Another band were also backstage and as usual, I started to chat with them *(I chat to anyone)*. I can't remember how it happened but we started to talk about body image and in particular being overweight. At one point in the conversation, one of the other band members mentioned that I was fat. I told them that it wasn't fat and that I suffer from cysts on my kidneys. I showed him the protrusion of my huge kidneys and he started to apologise. I told him that it is like being permanently pregnant and we both laughed it off. I do miss that backstage banter. The conversation inspired me to write this poem.

I'm Not Fat

I hear you laugh; you think that I'm fat
It's rather sad, as a matter of fact
You say, look at that bloke, he's so large
What a joke, he's the size of a barge
If you knew, what I've been through
I mean really been through
You certainly wouldn't mock
If you knew, what's really true
You would be in shock
So, let's take stock
of why I look like a bus
I don't fuss
don't eat too much
but the truth MUST, be told
I'm not big because I'm old
Though, I am getting on a bit
Clothes are hard to fit
but **I'm NOT fat,** that's a fact
Yes, I'm over-sized

guess why and win a prize.
If you give in, then I win
even with my double-chin
I'll put you out of your misery
And tell you why, I'm a plus-sized me
My kidneys are gigantic and I mean MEGA
A diet won't help, I'm like it forever
Polycystic Kidney Disease, is the medical name
If you could know what it's like
you'd never laugh again
I know that you don't mean it
when you laugh and grin
As underneath my skin
there's a mass that lies within

But God made me the way that I am
It was all part of His Master plan
I know that I'm big and not a pretty sight
But I still have fight
and the might to write
God spoke to me and said
"I've not finished with you yet."
The pen is mightier than the sword
I'm a ready-writer, that God has called
I'm not really fat, I just look that way
You may, think I'm a prat
but for you I pray
That's a fact and **I'm NOT FAT**

Why am I telling you all this now? The reason is that obesity can be an underlying factor for many other serious health issues. I had been waking up in the night for many months struggling to breathe. My snoring had increased to an extreme level of decibels and Heather told me that she would watch me sleep and every so often I stopped breathing.   I was falling asleep throughout the day as a result of such a bad night's sleep.

Once again, I was having tests and in May 2021 I was diagnosed with severe and complex sleep apnoea. Sleep apnoea can be caused by chemical (drug-induced) or mechanical (body) issues and I had both. I was told that on average I stopped breathing every 45 seconds, that's 90 times an hour, all through the night and needed to use a special machine to keep me breathing at night. I now sleep every night with a mask that covers my mouth and nose, with a tube that feeds a continuous flow of air.

As obesity is on the increase, so too is sleep apnoea, with 6% of the population affected. This still seems a low percentage and the problem is easily remedied with the machine, so for many it really doesn't seem a very big deal. For me though, on top of everything else that I suffer with, I questioned God, "Why me? Why is it always me?"

The next thing that I did was write this.

One more piece of straw!

On top of all my other health issues I fear
I am now diagnosed with sleep apnoea!
So now I know why I'm tired all the time.
And they tell me that I'll be just fine.
One more condition on my list.
A poor position, do you get my drift?
Let me give you the gist!
It's one more thing, on top of everything.
Am I supposed to do something?
I do the most I can do, I get creating.
Writing, biting off what I can chew,
that's what I do.
I keep it real, I know the deal,
you may know how I feel.
I'm not crying, long way from dying,
I know I'm not flying, but still.
I don't feel ill,
just tired, yet still inspired, maybe even admired?

I'm inspired to write this,
it's just one more condition on my list.
A poor position, do you get my drift?
Are you now getting the gist?
Can I take any more, it's just one more,
piece of straw
It won't break my back, I'm not a camel.
As a matter of fact, I'm a man-type mammal!
I'm spouting all my flannel!
When the going gets tough the weak run away?
Well, I'm gonna stay, not going, not today.
Did I hear you say, HOORAY?
It's just another diagnosis,
another one on my list.
Don't get me wrong, I don't dismiss,
I just persist, to exist.
Don't let it take the…
what did you expect?
A little defect, but I'm not a reject,
I have no regrets
At least now I know, way to go!
So let's get on with the show!
Just one more condition on my list.
A poor position, do you get my drift?
Do you now get the gist?

Whatever you face, and you've had enough.
Remember, get going when the going gets tough!

After writing this poem I felt better – I still felt valued. If you are wondering how just writing a poem can help, well consider this. In 2021 an interesting study was published by the American Academy of Paediatrics. They were assessing the behaviour of a group of 44 hospitalised children. The patients were encouraged to read and write poetry. The researchers saw reductions in fear, sadness, anger, worry and fatigue. The evidence concluded that poetry was a welcome distraction from stress and an opportunity for self-reflection. Poetry, or indeed any form of creative writing, will help to improve your mental health.

I believe that this is so important to all of us if we want to start to feel better about ourselves, especially if we want to understand that we are valued. Who doesn't want that? So, the reflective *(and entirely optional)* element for this chapter is similar to the last chapter. This is just me trying to encourage you to be creative.

Consider this...

1. Create something with your own hands, a
    painting, drawing, textile, a garden or a
    special cake.

    Pray first and allow the Holy Spirit to
    guide you to your creative self.

2. Share your creation with at least one
    person.

    If you are able, share it with a larger
    group.

3. Accept the positive comments and allow
    them to inspire you to create even more.

Chapter Fifteen
Put your 'Blest' foot forward

In June 2022, I published my 9th book, Legacy of the Mimics. I published another poetry book later on in August that year. This brought my total to ten books so far. This is quite a significant achievement for any writer, although for me, with so many health hurdles that I had to contend with, I regard it as miraculous.

As with any miracle, there is a natural tendency to want to share your story and so I looked for opportunities. I had previously made several attempts at pushing myself out there. I'd look for any events to speak at and especially perform poetry, but it had been fruitless. I felt the Holy Spirit nudge me in this direction for years but self-promotion does seem a most unnatural thing to do.

A year earlier in 2021, I was struggling with this so much that I was inspired once again to write. As you may have gathered by now, it's what I do to try to stabilise my feelings and my mental well-being. This time I wrote...

No Honour

In Nazareth, the Nazarene,
was never believed and rarely seen.
I know a little of how it must have been,
for the Nazarene.
As those at the scene, think that I'm obscene.
But really, I am not, I'm a man of honour.
Speaking truth upon ya.
Not in it for profit.
Don't do it to fill my pocket.
No Shakespearian sonnet
Hurt, but get back on it.
Love? I want it.
Attraction of the opposite
Will you ever drop it?
Simply catastrophic.
Make me want to vomit.
No honour for the Prophet.

Not in my back yard, it really is so hard.
Disbelief, need relief
Need hope, yes, hope.
Instead you treat me like a joke.
But I'm not laughing.
Simply asking why?
Why can't you give me a chance.

Not asking for a romance.
Allow my words to enhance.
Time now to advance.
I'm a prophet without honour,
in the town where I was born.
They treat me like a bomber
and they pierce me with a thorn.
And I? I just mourn.
No need for a storm
I just feel down.
Mourn for the town
and for the lost.
Because I do give a toss.
I care about them regardless.
A prophet without honour nevertheless.
I care about them, like the Nazarene
But when they look at me, they see Frankenstein.
Now I know that this isn't true for all,
And this does give me hope.
Pride it comes before a fall,
Get off that slippery slope.

Like a dog with a bone, I wouldn't give up
gnawing away at it. I knew that God was
directing my path, so continued to look for
opportunities. So, in June 2022, I searched for a
Christian book festival anywhere in the UK. I
found plenty in the USA and one that had

happened once, as a one-off event in the UK but nothing existed.

I instantly felt that there was a huge need for a Christian book festival and I knew plenty of authors that would be glad to take part. I felt God leading me, speaking into my heart, **"I have given you tools and skills to use."**

I felt that God was calling me to start a festival, so I, first of all, tried the easy option and asked the well-established, *'Stroud Book Festival'* if we could provide a Christian venue as part of their festival. This would mean that we could be included in all of their advertising. I thought that it was a good idea but it wasn't God's idea, God doesn't particularly like the easy option.

Do not be unequally bound together with unbelievers
[do not make mismatched alliances with them,
inconsistent with your faith]. For what partnership can
righteousness have with lawlessness? Or what
fellowship can light have with darkness?
2 Corinthians 6:14 (Amplified Bible).

I waited for a response but none arrived. A restlessness stirred in my heart and I became agitated. I describe it as having a stone in your shoe, it gives you discomfort and sooner or later you are going to have to remove the shoe. I eased the irritation by searching for a venue. I figured, that when the Stroud Book Festival people eventually came back to me, I could tell them that I have a venue.

I also need to point out that the festival is held annually in November, so there was already less than four months to put it all together. I had organised festivals and events in the past and I knew that this would be difficult in the time available. If it was going to happen, it would take a miracle.

I aimed to find the four different key elements that we would need.

- The venue, as already mentioned
- A keynote speaker
- Some authors, of course and
- The necessary funding.

I knew that we would need at least three months to advertise the festival, once these things were in place, so only had a month to secure all these.

I sent one email to one church and almost

immediately the Reverend Keith Rudman caught the vision. He allowed us to use Stroud Baptist Church at no cost. It was such a generous offer.

At the end of the same week, I posted a call out for Christian authors. I advertised this on the Association of Christian Authors page and their members too caught the vision. I aimed for fourteen writers in total and by the end of the weekend the response had been incredible. All of the spaces had been filled and we even had a reserve list. The call-out had attracted authors from all over the UK, from hundreds of miles away. I knew that there was a need for this event because there was nothing else like it, but I had never anticipated this level of response. I began to sense a real excitement building for this festival – a Holy Spirit buzz.

Two of the four essential requirements had been found in less than a week, which is enough to make anyone tingle with excitement. However, finding a keynote speaker was going to be a more difficult task and so I needed to find some help. Mike Juggins, the owner of Scrolleaters Christian bookshop, was keen to help, as was the Reverend Jo Regan *(she loves reading does she)*. Both of these two made some wonderful suggestions, coming up with names that I would never have imagined.

Sophie Neville was suggested by Jo and I was already in contact with her through social media and the Association of Christian Writers. I chatted briefly with Sophie, agreed on a suitable fee and booked her to appear on the Friday evening of the 1st Stroud Christian Book Festival. It had taken about two weeks to reach this stage.

Three out of four of the needs had been met. I had stepped out in faith but next came what could possibly be considered the biggest step of faith, we needed money. For that first year, we were able to work within a budget of £700. I launched a crowdfunding appeal and wrote to the local churches and a few Christian businesses. Miraculously the full amount had been pledged within a month of finding the venue. The four essential needs had been found and during that crazy whirlwind month, I even managed to buy a domain name and build a website. Things had happened so fast and I never expected that. Then, I suddenly realised, we didn't have a bank account. How were we supposed to receive the funds?

I made several enquiries and eventually settled on

the bank that I already banked with, one of the main high street banks. The application was a quick process but there were two stages of approval. The first stage could take up to a week and the second stage another month. More faith was needed so I prayed and asked Jo Regan to pray. The first stage was approved the next day and the whole account was open within six days. God had worked another miracle and we were now officially in business.

After three weeks of contacting the Stroud Book Festival, they eventually responded and politely turned us down. They didn't want a Christian venue as part of their festival. I thought it only fair to tell them that they had taken so long to respond, that we had already progressed with our own festival and that it would sit alongside theirs. They were happy to hear that and we were happy not to be yoked to them.

Up until that stage, we had been using the same branding colours as Stroud Book Festival, and the team of Jo, Mike and I, now felt a need to differentiate. We discussed various suggestions for a name for the festival and settled on **BOOK BLEST Christian book festival.**

On the 4th and 5th of November 2022, the very first Book Blest festival took place and it was regarded as a great success. We were learning as we stepped out in faith on this new venture and God provided all of our needs.

At the outset, I had established what I considered to be the aims of this festival. Primarily we wanted to give God the glory for giving us the ability to create and especially write. Our other aims had been to act as a festival of excellence and opportunity for all Christian authors. We also wanted to bring hope, encouragement and inspiration to those writers and for them to know that they are not alone. Finally, we felt that it was important to show the world that God is real, relevant and relational.

The feedback that we received confirmed that we had achieved the vision and our mission now continues. At the end of the festival, we immediately started to plan for the next year and beyond. The greater vision is to see this event replicated in towns across the UK, to give more opportunity to more Christian authors and to continue to glorify God in our writing. I recently heard from someone who lives in Northern Ireland and attended the first Book Blest. She was so impressed and inspired, that she has now started a Christian writers and book fair in her home town.

For me personally, Book Blest boosted my confidence and encouraged me to push myself out there more. This has resulted in numerous bookings and speaking engagements. These mainly feature my testimony and poetry. I am excited about the prospect of my venues and events and am open to wherever God leads me. I may have multiple health issues and invisible disabilities, yet I am still able, and capable and yes, you guessed it, I'm still valued and so are you.

Consider this...

1. Pray about setting up a Book Blest festival in your town.

2. Contact Book Blest, Stroud so that we can help you. www.bookblest.co.uk

3. Find a team and start to find the four essential needs – venue, authors, keynote

speaker (you can always ask me) and funding.

Chapter Sixteen
The deepest valley

There is a thought that many Christians believe, when we step out to work for the glory of God, we can come under attack. I believe that is true. If and when we step onto the battlefield, casualties are possible. I say this because I have experienced it so many times that when it happens, it isn't a surprise. Often, for me, I can struggle with weariness and fatigue leading up to or after an event. You could say that this is only to be expected given my health issues. Then, during an event, I feel spiritually supercharged as a supernatural filling occurs. You could argue that this is adrenalin surging through my body, but I say this is how God equips us for the battle. This is how He strengthens us with the endurance to run the race that He has set out before us.

This is the story of the toughest battle that I have ever faced and I am currently still coping with the aftermath. The memories are fresh and the ordeal was brutal. It was the deepest, darkest valley that I have survived and I know that I was not alone. I know that He was by my side.

Psalm 23 means so much more to me now, as does this poem that I wrote a few years ago.

Valley

As I walk through the valley
of the shadow of death
I don't feel fear, I feel your caress
I excite, that I might
see you this day
Then in spite, of my plight
I delight to pray
And you hear, hold me dear
near to keep me safe
From the grave, I stay brave
feel your love embrace
In my darkest depression
hear my heartfelt confession
In my tearful expression
you leave a lasting Impression
Now, in my deep despair
I feel your presence there
like you care
Despite the pain I face
you wrap me in your grace
Say run the race
set the pace

but my pace is slow
Darkness brings a deathblow

Show, me which way to go
I hear you say hello
Time to follow
yet, I feel so hollow
so I wallow in the mire
No desire
lost my fire
life soon expire
await my funeral pyre
When life is tough
I've had enough
feel like giving up
It's then he kicks my butt
my eyes had been shut
My open eyes
to my surprise
remove the disguise of night
I rise, to the prize, of light
a glorious sight
You lift me, from the valley
Saying, this is not your finale

It had been twenty-one months since I had felt
any angina pains and I had done my best to get
on with life. I have felt that pain so many times,

it is like recognising a familiar friend, in this case not a very nice friend – not really a friend at all. It starts *(for me)* as a slight numbness, a niggle in my wrist. It morphs into an ache, escalating, and a warning is sent to my brain, this is pain. At first, it moves slowly up my arms and then it crosses my chest. I question, "Why are you back?"

I have another friend; a nice friend and I keep him in my pocket. I direct the nozzle of the little red bottle underneath my tongue and spray. It didn't work and so I spray again. Still, I am in pain. I don't want to be so I spray the GTN spray a third time. The rules state that if I need to spray three times, I need to call for an ambulance. I wait, the pain subsides, the spray has worked, no need for an ambulance, this is not an emergency, this is my reasoning.

After a short rest, I resume whatever I was doing, it was something physical. It's always physical exercise that triggers the pain. It had been happening for a few weeks and it was beginning to worsen, with more serious pain and more often but the GTN spray did the trick. Even though it was taking longer to work, at least it worked.

It had started a few weeks before Christmas, about a month after the Book Blest festival. Christmas came and went along with Boxing Day, a restful time. Then, on 27th December 2022, I woke at 2.00am with pain. I felt pinned to the bed and couldn't move, so Heather grabbed my GTN spray. Three squirts and it eventually eased. Exhausted, I fell back into a deep sleep until 7.00am. It had only been five hours and I knew what I had to do. My angina had become unstable. Unstable angina is unreliable and the most dangerous type. I spent most of the morning trying to speak to a doctor. The emergency services were overwhelmed and the phone systems not working correctly. It was 2.00pm by the time I arrived in the Emergency Department of Cheltenham General Hospital, where I would remain for the next 48 hours.

After two nights, I woke on the second morning with severe pain in the toes of my right foot. It was agonising and diagnosed as chronic gout, caused by dehydration and my underlying renal failure. The pain was so bad that I struggled to walk and for a short period, but it took my mind off of the more serious issue.

Everything in the hospital takes time, x-rays, blood tests, ECG, general observations, monitoring, and medication. Time passed extremely slowly but eventually, I was given a bed in the cardiology ward.

I was immediately given a five-day course of eight steroids a day to fight off the gout. I am pretty sure that this also gave me the strength that my heart needed and I felt very little pain for about a week. I began to feel a little like a fraud and that I was taking up a bed unnecessarily. I waited about two days before finding out just how serious my situation was. I needed an angiogram, a procedure that involves inserting a catheter into an artery in the groin, arm or neck. It is threaded through the blood vessels to the heart. A coronary angiogram can show blocked or narrowed blood vessels in the heart and uses X-ray imaging and a special dye *(contrast)* to see your heart's blood vessels.

This would be my fourth angiogram; two of the previous times had resulted in having six coronary stents inserted to keep my arteries flowing and each time the dye had lowered my kidney function. It was always something of a trade-off, improved heart health at the cost of my renal condition.

I'm gowned up and wheeled to a freezing cold lab where blankets are piled on top of me, as I lay on a surgical table. I am conscious throughout the procedure and I recognise the familiar feelings of prodding and poking. The Cardiologist talks to me, reassuring me, and then he stops, the investigation is over, now he will tell me the news.

"You have some serious blockage to three of your arteries. They are very difficult to reach. We could fix it with stents but they wouldn't last much longer than 18 months. We need to discuss the best way forward with the surgeons."

I struggled to take it all in and a surge of emotion caused the tears to well up. When I returned to the ward the nurses were surprised to hear the news as I didn't appear to be ill. Their reaction made it seem even more real and I knew then that I was facing a triple bypass – open heart surgery.

I knew many others who had gone down this treacherous road including my dad, mum and brother. I had witnessed their struggles but had no idea of the level of pain and suffering that lay ahead. I tried to stay positive, I tried to write... but it was not easy. I wrote this before my surgery.

Bad News

Bad news arrives
I decide to try to stop the slide,
the subside
Into the divide so wide
I take care to avoid the despair,
lingering just there
I fail
It surrounds, all around, as my soul is bound
I scream aloud, muffled by darkness shroud
Covered, smothered, food for the Buzzard
I tumble and stumble into the divide,
look to the skies
Try to get a grip, as I slip into the miry pit
More bad news crushes my head
Filled with dread, depression being fed
Let it in, under my skin, will I ever win?
In a bad news spin, lights are dim
Things aren't great
Help me to escape
Before it's too late

No time to debate
What is my fate
Just need a mate
Before it's too late
To listen and care,
To lift me from despair
Is there anyone there?

I stayed in the ward in Cheltenham until a bed could be found at the Bristol Heart Institute. Each day that I waited my pains were increasing, more frequent, more severe, lasting longer and mainly at night. I cried out to God and questioned Him, "Why am I here? Why is this happening?" Then I started to speak in to the opportunities that arose.

On New Year's Eve, I wrote a poem and dedicated it to the nurses and staff. I recorded it as a spoken word video and posted it on my YouTube channel *(all from my hospital bed)*. I performed the poem to other patients and visitors. I had numerous conversations about being a Christian and at one point I even performed one of my old rap songs. Why was I here? The answer is always the same, no matter where you are. The answer is, to be wholly available and ready to be used by God. Even whilst seriously ill and waiting for major heart surgery, God chooses to use me and He will do the same for you because you are still valued.

Consider this...

1. Are you struggling with a difficult situation?

   Do you question where God is in all of it?

   Discuss how you are feeling with a friend or group.

2. Wherever you are and whatever you are facing, ask God why you are there and expect an answer.

3. Offer yourself to God, ask Him to use you and say, "Here I am Lord, wholly available.

Chapter Seventeen
Endurance

I spent a total of two weeks in Cheltenham Cardiology Ward and on the day that I was due to leave they tested me for any communicable diseases. My Covid test was negative but I had an indicator for Flu. On arrival in Bristol, they put me in isolation with a sign on the door, 'Flu Infection Control.'

A nurse quickly did my general observations, then hastily left. For a few hours, it seemed as if I was being ignored, I mean, who wants to catch Flu? Someone later brought me a sandwich and a cup of tea. Then, I later found out that some of my paperwork was missing and they were, therefore, uncertain how to process me.

The Flu is exhausting and I eventually went to bed very late. I must have slept for about three hours before being woken abruptly with chest pain, at about 2.00am. It was serious pain and I struggled to move to reach the call bell. The attack was the worst that I have ever experienced and took lots of GTN to make it subside.

After a routine ECG, I fell back to sleep until the same happened again at about 4.00am and 6.00am. This time, after the ECG, I was asked to sign a consent form, met with the anesthetist and was prepped for theatre. The nurse shaved my chest, arms and legs. She explained that I had been bumped up the list for an emergency operation and told me to advise my family.

I called Heather and told her. In the hurry, I had forgotten to hang up the phone and left the line open. She could hear me talking as I was taken to the operating theatre. I remember multiple cannulas being fitted, and then my body started to feel fuzzy and the lights dimmed. I woke up two days later.

I had been on a life-support machine since surgery, which was a familiar experience. As before, they woke me up with the tube still down my throat. It really is a disorientating and disempowering experience. I wanted to ask questions, but couldn't. When the tube was eventually removed the first thing that I asked for was pain relief. I couldn't move, I didn't want to, the pain was more than anything that I had previously experienced. A device with a red button was placed into my hand and the nurse instructed me to press it. The pain was reduced with the injection of morphine, but it was still bad.

I was in an isolation room because of the Flu and a nurse never left my side. He was so reassuring and explained everything to me. I couldn't see the monitors and the stack of equipment that my body was connected to, as it was located behind me. Later that day when Heather arrived with Steve Woodcock, they described it to me. Their faces looked shocked by the sight before them.

The morphine messes with my memory but I do remember every day I vomited a lot, I struggled to keep food down. Every day more tubes were removed from my body as progress was made, but I still battled with pain.

The decision was made to stop my morphine and give me Fentanyl, a far more powerful opioid and easier going on my kidneys. Fentanyl is approximately 100 times more potent than morphine and 50 times more potent than heroin as an analgesic. It certainly was extremely efficient at stopping pain and in the space of 24 hours, I pressed the little red button enough times to inject three whole syringes into my body.

It just so happens that delirium is one of the side effects of this potent drug. The feeling is rather pleasant and very similar to morphine. I felt relaxed and at ease, sleepy and as if I was floating. I can't recall how long I had been on Fentanyl when the hallucinations started. At first, they were quite enjoyable, euphoric even. In my tiredness, I closed my eyes and immediately found myself in what I can only describe as an alternate reality. I use the word reality because that is how it felt – REAL.

I was transported to a joyful place full of fun and had a great time sliding down huge sand dunes. It was amazing and felt so real. After a while, I opened my eyes and I found myself back in my bed, in my isolation room with a nurse by my side. I briefly closed my eyes and was transported back, then opened them and returned. Through this action, I had the belief that I could control the journey between the two realities. After numerous trips to the sand dunes, confusion set in and I struggled to determine what was real and what wasn't.

Eventually, I found myself trapped in the alternate place. I remember someone telling me that I had to be on the transport to return by midnight, but I was enjoying being there so much that I didn't want it to end, so I stayed. I heard the chime of a clock indicating that it was midnight and saw a car whizz past me with people escaping. At that moment, I was sucked into a wall and became a concrete figurine in a grotesque grotto. I tried to move and cry out, but I was trapped. Fear began to fill my thoughts and it seemed to last forever.

Eventually, my eyes opened and I was back in my bed. I'm not sure how I had been behaving in my unconscious state but the nurse looked a little concerned. I closed my eyes for a moment and nothing happened, I felt safe. The hallucinations had stopped... I hadn't been pressing my little red button.

As I returned to reality, so too did the pain, so I pressed the button. Every time I was allowed, I pressed it. Soon a new reality appeared whenever I closed my eyes. This time I saw a basic computer screen. It looked very similar to a spreadsheet and was mainly green. In the top left was a large green button with the word 'exit'. I watched the mouse arrow move toward it and click it. I opened my eyes and was back to reality.

I visited this computer screen reality several times before I was once again, trapped. This time the cage was different. As I opened my eyes expecting to return to the room, I could still see the computer screen, the two realities had merged.

The screen was on the wall. On the left were letters and at the top a communication box. I could see the mouse arrow and wondered if I could control it. The usual hospital table stretched across my bed in front of me. I placed my right hand on the table and moved it. The mouse moved with it. I was in control. With my left finger, I tapped the table and found out that I could click and select letters. I was watching the screen on the wall opposite me and a nurse was watching me.

I typed words like 'hello' into the box until I could no more. Somehow my mouse disappeared, just like it does in reality, only I couldn't find it. In reality, we always eventually find it but it was impossible. I felt trapped again.

I frantically tried to find the mouse, one hand

sliding, the other tapping on the table. I thought to myself, "If only I could click the exit button, as I had before, then I could escape." I was biting on my tongue with the anxiety and the nurse called for help.

I tried to explain in a calm manner, "I know what you are thinking. You think that I'm having a fit, but I'm not. I just need to find my mouse. Can you see it?" I asked, as I stared at the wall opposite. She seemed even more confused than me.

Suddenly, words started to materialise in the communication box, and slowly they faded in and out. Slowly they calmed me down. **"YOU... ARE... DYING."** It should have been alarming but instead, I just had peace.

I read each word out loud, then questioned who said that. One word appeared in the box, **"GOD."**

Shocked and stunned, I spoke out loud again, "Is that really you God? Am I really dying?"

"YES... YES", came the reply.

"I'm dying", I said quietly, then I asked the nurse, "Have my family been called." To which she replied, "Yes."

"Wow, I'm talking to God", I said. The nurse looked at me as if I was bonkers. "Where am I going, God?" I wanted to know.

"STANDBY... DESTINATION... COMING UP......HEAVEN"

"Wow, I'm dying and I'm going to heaven", I spoke quieter as a peace filled me. Then, without any prompt, words that listed my life's work appeared.

"THE DOOR... MASTER'S MC... POETRY... GOLDEN... THREAD..." and other books appeared. There were many things mentioned and I can't remember them all. This was my life before my eyes.

Suddenly, I wondered how I could let Heather know about this conversation, so I asked and the answer came on the screen, which only I could see.

"JESUS..." she would know because Jesus

would tell her.

Just then, I thought that I needed to see my family before I died, so I asked the nurse when they would arrive.

I'm not sure why the nurse had previously answered 'yes' when I asked if my family had been called. Now she told me, "It's two o'clock in the morning. You are not dying and we cannot phone them."

More words appeared on my screen and I repeated them, shouting them out in desperation. **"LIES... CONSPIRACY... TREACHERY..."**

At some point, another nurse entered. She had been waiting for a doctor to prescribe some medication. The anti-psychotic worked quickly, it calmed me down and the computer screen on the wall faded, and then it was no more. The brain is a powerful organ and my conversation with God felt so real. Was it real? Who knows, but I can recall so much of it, which, it seems is rather unusual.

I closed my eyes and saw traces of green lines, like the green 'code rain' in the film, 'The Matrix.

I quietly whispered to myself, "Wow, I'm in The Matrix." The lines disappeared and I think I slept briefly. As I slept, I saw the typical scene that many people have talked about. I was in a tunnel that was lit with light. People waited in a queue and made their way towards an even brighter light. I didn't recognise anyone. I remember thinking, surely, I must know someone.

I awoke and the nurse smiled at me. I smiled back and drifted off again. The same happened again, the same scene. Again, I didn't recognise anyone and I didn't feel as if I belonged there. I assumed it just wasn't my time and the scene faded. I must have slept for the rest of the night and awoke to find the day nurse was back looking after me. I was so pleased to see him, it felt normal and real.

What seemed to be a close brush with death or a near-death experience (NDE) left me feeling extremely emotional. I still feel that same emotion months after surgery. When Heather arrived later that day, I shared my experience with her. I struggled through tears. I shared the same story with others and now, I have shared it with you. It really was an incredibly believable experience, but I am so glad to be alive.

The next day, despite still being infectious with the Flu, my regular day nurse asked me if I would like to go outside. I relished it, even though I knew that the January air would be bitterly cold. So, he sat me in a wheelchair and smothered me with blankets. My face was obscured with a mask, so I must have looked a very odd sight, with just a pair of blue eyes peering out from the blue blankets.

Once outside I could remove my mask. The cold air was exhilarating. The nurse told me to look up between the buildings and see the sky. There was a reason for all that he did for me. This time, because I had been in the hospital for nearly three weeks, my body needed sunlight and vitamin D. As I glanced toward heaven, snow started to land on my face and I was overwhelmed by the emotion. Tears and mucus flowed freely as the nurse handed me some tissues. He was prepared. He had seen it in many patients before, but I wondered how many of them thought that they were dying. How many were feeling the joy that I now felt?

It had been a slow road to recovery and I was

discharged from the hospital with a serious chest infection. Months later, after antibiotics, I am still suffering the effects of that infection and I am still taking regular pain relief.

Less than two months after surgery, I spoke at the Full Gospel Businessmen's dinner in Bath and God used me. He is still using me and I still feel valued.

I still fight health battles every day and expect to do so for the rest of my life. Less than three months after my heart surgery, I was admitted to the hospital with a chronic kidney infection. It is not unusual for someone with polycystic kidneys, but this was my first kidney infection. After another week, lots of prayer and antibiotics, plus of course more sharing of my faith with the nurses, I was allowed to go home.

Consider this...

1. Thank God for the endurance that He gives you to persevere.

2. Start to list the blessings that you have in your life, especially the little things like sunshine and a snowflake on your skin.

3. Think again about someone who is struggling with health or other issues and befriend them. My nurse was like a lifeline to me.

Chapter Eighteen
The future?

The stories in this book may make you wonder whether my life is like one long drama. After all, my tales are rather dramatic. I am pleased to say that I do experience long moments of peace between the battles, though even on peaceful days, I live with the symptoms of a broken body. This is my normal. Twenty pills a day and a constant supply of morphine *(I wear a pain patch)*, help to maintain my normal. I praise God for the peaceful, average days, the mundane days, without any form of crisis. I thank God for every day that I have breath in my lungs and regard each as a bonus. It may sound strange to say it, but I am also grateful for the difficult days, for every scuffle, conflict and battle; the big and the small ones. I think of the caterpillar that has to fight with all their might, just to get out of their cocoon. All this, merely to stay alive and move into the next stage of metamorphosis. Without any struggle, there would be no beautiful creation, such as this emerging butterfly. Their wings wouldn't have become strong enough to fly and so they'd soon die.

My health skirmishes actually inspire me to create. Words are my weapon of choice. How do you fight your battles? What inspires your creativity?

What does the future hold for any of us? How can any one of us answer that question with 100% certainty? I know 100% that I am going to heaven, although I don't know when. Who does?

My experience of stepping out of my gate and being hit by a speeding cyclist tells me that the unexpected happens. My triple heart bypass tells me to be prepared for the worst. My God tells me that I am still valued. How do I know that? Quite simply because He keeps using me as His instrument. As long I say, "Here I am Lord wholly available", I know that He will continue to show me more of what He wants me to do.

Ultimately, He wants each one of us to have a deeper, more meaningful relationship. He wants us to spend time with Him, to chat with Him, to listen to Him and be obedient to His desire for each one of us.

We all fail dismally with this as we are distracted

by other tasks and hindrances. We allow our selfish desires to sideline the will of God for our lives. We are all guilty of this. As mentioned earlier in this book, I wrote the book of 'Psalms in Rhyme' alongside writing 'One God Many Names.' At the time, I was saturated in scripture and I felt this was the closest that I have ever been to God. I want you to experience some of that.

What does the future hold? I want that Psalms experience again. I want it more and more. I want to communicate with God on a daily basis, 24 hours a day, 7 days a week. I want conversations just like I had when I was under the influence of mind-altering substances. Yet, we don't need drugs to achieve this. Romans 12:2 says, *'We are being transformed by the renewing of our minds.'*

What does the future hold? I want my mind to be transformed.

I want to push myself out of my comfort zone and beyond, to get out of my comfortable boat and walk on metaphoric water. Is that what you want?

The Reverend Steve Chalke used to ask this question. If you could know what God is doing and be part of it, would you want to? Some of you may say, "Yes, I want to know." Others may say, "Yes, I want to be part of it, whatever it is." How many will say, "Yes I want to know and be part of it, no matter what it is."

You may have already heard the story of tightrope walker Charles Blondin. He stretched a tightrope over a quarter of a mile, spanning the breadth of Niagara Falls. The thundering sound of the pounding water drowning out all other sounds is fearful enough, but then he stepped onto the rope and walked across.

This stunning act made Blondin famous in the summer of 1859. Several times, he walked 160 feet above the falls, back and forth between Canada and the United States as huge crowds on both sides looked on with shock and awe. Once he crossed in a sack, once on stilts, another time on a bicycle and once he even carried a stove and cooked an omelette.

On July 15, Blondin walked backwards across the tightrope to Canada and returned pushing a wheelbarrow.

The story is told that it was after pushing the wheelbarrow across again, this time while blindfolded, that Blondin asked for some audience participation. The crowds had watched with great expectation. He had proved that he could do it and they all believed in him; of that, there was no doubt. Then, he asked his audience, "Do you believe I can carry a person across in this wheelbarrow?"

"Of course", the crowd shouted back, "Yes, you can do it, we believe."

However, when he asked for a volunteer to get into the wheelbarrow and take a ride across the Falls with him, no one came forward.

Later in August of 1859, his manager, Harry Colcord, did ride on Blondin's back across the Falls.

This story is sadly very similar to our Christian lives, we say that we believe but do we have faith? Are you ready to put your trust in God for whatever future lies ahead for you?

Proverbs 3:5-6 says,
'Trust in the LORD with all your heart and
do not lean on your own understanding.
In all your ways acknowledge Him and
He will make your paths straight.'

Lack of trust and doubt are massive barriers that hold us back. Low self-worth, disbelief and imposter syndrome will prevent you from achieving what God has planned for you. Another barrier is apathy and I see it all around me. Humanity is infected with it. I say 'infected' because I have seen it spread like a deadly contagion.

If you don't believe me, try asking for volunteers for a worthy cause and take a look at how society has changed in the last ten years. In 2012/13, 70% of people volunteered at least once a year and 44% at least once a month. Those figures have since fallen to 55% and 34% respectfully.

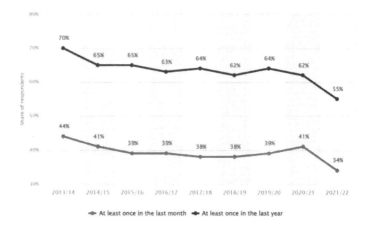

Whatever your future holds, I urge you to consider volunteering your time and skills. This will help you to understand that you are still valued. I am pretty sure that I have already mentioned that a few times, but do you believe it? Do you realise that God looks at you in a completely different way? He sees your potential. He wants to use your strengths, that is obvious, but he can also turn your weaknesses into His opportunities. If that makes you fearful, don't worry He can also eliminate any threats.

This next poem is a bit of a riddle, you already know the answer. The question is, are you a prisoner?

Prisoners

These people are so dumb
Deluded by their so-called freedom
They are secluded as my captive
Restrained from being active
My invisible bonds are wound tight
They don't fight, no need to show my sight
I don't use fright to capture my prey
I simply delight them to stray
From what is right and how to pray
My prisoner puppets avoid all action
My weapon of choice is simple distraction
I steal their voices fraction by fraction
I tempt them with subtle attraction
I fill them with self-satisfaction
I am the killer of vision
Destroyer of mission
I take one life at a time
I deceive, you believe all is fine
I am jailer of the multitude
The never failure to intrude
You know who I am
I am all around
Wherever you look
I am found
Do you know who I am?

Will you have a guess?
I know you can
But you don't care less
I am the captive taker
Church breaker
World shaker
You are slave to me
You will never see
I am apathy
You know my name
I am the bad stain
I am always there
And you don't care
You are my prisoners under my spell
You all believe that all is well

As I come to the end of my story so far, I hear
the news that Christian singer-songwriter, Dave
Bryant has just passed away. I am certain that he
is now spending eternity in the glory of God.
One of the songs that Dave penned was 'Jesus
take me as I am' and I wonder how many of us
pray these words and really mean them. Look at
some of the other words.

Jesus take me as I am
I can come no other way
Take me deeper into you

Make my flesh life melt away

Make me like a precious stone
Crystal clear and finely honed
Love of Jesus shining through
Giving glory back to you

Can you say these words and really mean them?
Do you want to go deeper with God? Will you
allow Him to hone you? We are all pretty much
like rough diamonds that have just been dug out
of the ground. We are not that impressive, yet
we have potential. Rough diamonds are covered
in filth, yet when they have been transformed, the
light sparkles from them. In our raw state, God
looks at each one of us and says, **"You are
valued and I take you as you are. Let me wash
away your flesh life as you come deeper into
me. You will be my instrument, my precious
stone."**

Not one of us can know clearly what the future
holds, there is just so much that cannot be
predicted or prepared for. We all face
uncertainty, but for me, I seem to have an
abundance of the unexpected. These are mainly
health-related. They could prevent me from
making plans. For example, if I agreed to be

somewhere and then ended up in the hospital again, I would be letting people down. Thoughts like this, but maybe not as extreme, do hold people back from making any commitments. Potentially this is preventing some people from being wholly available, to be used by God.

Of course, I don't want to let people down, but more importantly, I don't want to let God down. So, I push myself out there, I knock on doors and I go to where God leads.

I continue to write however God leads me and I am open to all of the opportunities that He reveals to me. I am now taking bookings for speaking engagements, which are mainly testimony and poetry. I am looking beyond the present and faithfully booking dates months in advance. I pray that God will watch over me and protect me and that He will use me to inspire and bless others. I hope that you have found my story inspiring and that you will now let God show you what to do next with your life.

Future

What does the future hold?
Would you like to be told?
What is around the next corner?
Do you want an informer?
To predict a verdict
To avoid conflict
To know what lies ahead
To know what will be said
Before it's said
Would it be good to know?
To know which way to go?
To know what will happen every hour
It would be like having a superpower
But life would be so predictable
No longer excitable
No surprises
No fun
Boring
We need a mix of fearlessly and fearfully
To live carelessly and purposefully
We need certain and uncertainty
We need a balance to enhance
To be still and dance
To walk and run
Variety is fun

Only God knows what the future holds
He watches as it unfolds
We simply behold

Consider this...

1. Start each day by praying for God to show you and lead you and say, "Here I am wholly available, make me like a precious stone."

2. Keep a list of your options and pray over them, asking God what He wants from you.

3. Keep a daily journal, you never know, your story could become a book to inspire.

Brendan Conboy has an active speaking
MINISTRY for GOD
And is looking forward to
hearing from you

Contact Brendan at the following:
Email – bmconboy@gmail.com
Phone - +44 (0)1453 731008
Mobile – 07980 404873
www.brendanconboy.co.uk

The following pages contain information
about Brendan's book titles (Bibliography).

The Golden Thread – Biography
A true story of fear, forgiveness and faith
First published – 1ˢᵗ September 2015

Brendan Conboy grew up in fear and confusion, struggling with many personal issues. These experiences formed a foundation that could have ended in disaster, but instead, became the motivator to want to make a positive difference.

Issues – Teen / YA Fiction
We all have issues… Can a bully change?
First published – 23ʳᵈ January 2019

Marcus Daniel was a caring, intelligent, larger-than-average ten-year-old. His parents changed and then so did he. Now Marcus is thirteen years old and a spiteful bully, full of anger, rage and pain. His actions have changed others. Will the fear, pain and rage win?

My Foundation for Life – Semi Biog / Scriptural Teaching
14 underpinning and impacting scriptures
First published – 19th February 2019

What is it that makes some of us more resilient than others? I am sure that psychologists will have several long-winded explanations to answer this question, but I believe that we can increase our resilience by building our lives on a foundation of truth

Rhyme Time – Poetry
Poems with a message for you to read.
Poems of truth that plant a seed.
First published – 13th November 2020

The Invasion of the MIMICS
Science Fiction / Dystopian / Fantasy
They're already here… Invading your country…
Dwelling in your home… Living in your body!
First published – 21ˢᵗ October 2020

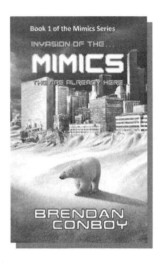

Climate change had been predicted long ago, but not one person could foresee the events that had unfolded. Humanity is defeated, civilization lost, all hope has gone. Enlightenment is the new belief, but there are those who refuse to believe.

The Land of Make Believe – Children's fantasy in rhyme
Based on the story of doubting Thomas
First published – 4ᵗʰ March 2021

ONE GOD Many Names
First published – 14th July 2021

When we meditate on the many names of God, something powerful can happen to us. Brendan Conboy shares his thoughts and personal stories of what some of these names mean and how they had a transformational impact on his life.

The Book of PSALMS in Rhyme
First published – 24th August 2021

POWERFUL...
POETIC...

RHYTHMIC, RHYMING PSALMS...

A fresh expression to ignite your soul.

Legacy of the Mimics
First published – 20th June 2022

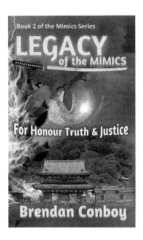

Book 2 in the Mimics series.
Her eyes told her everything was calm, as it should be. Her eyes deceived her. Her mind sensed something else.

Beyond the void

Popcorn Poetry
First published – 30th August 2022

75 Poems that pop with rhythm & rhyme
The concept of
Popcorn Poetry is simple, popcorn is made for sharing, just like the rhymes in this book - read them out loud and share them with friends.

Half Man Half Poet
First published – 2nd April 2023

An enzyme of rhyme designed for this time
Life – Health – Social issues – Christian message. This book has something for everyone

The End is not The End
First published – June 2023

Poems for end of life and beyond – There is no avoiding death, it happens to us all. These poems will hopefully bring peace in the struggle.

The Gift
First published 25th Sptember 2023

A compilation of 4 of my poetry books.

Rhyme Time

Popcorn Poetry

Half Man

The End

Printed in Great Britain
by Amazon

29893204R00110